CW00925665

St Ninian and the Earliest Christianity in Scotland

Papers from the conference held
by The Friends of the Whithorn Trust
in Whithorn on September 15th 2007

Edited by

Jane Murray

BAR British Series 483
2009

This title published by

Archaeopress
Publishers of British Archaeological Reports
Gordon House
276 Banbury Road
Oxford OX2 7ED
England
bar@archaeopress.com
www.archaeopress.com

BAR 483

St Ninian and the Earliest Christianity in Scotland: Papers from the conference held by The Friends of the Whithorn Trust in Whithorn on September 15th 2007

© Archaeopress and the individual authors 2009

ISBN 978 1 4073 0428 1

Printed in England by Blenheim Colour Ltd

All BAR titles are available from:

Hadrian Books Ltd
122 Banbury Road
Oxford
OX2 7BP
England
bar@hadrianbooks.co.uk

The current BAR catalogue with details of all titles in print, prices and means of payment is available free from Hadrian Books or may be downloaded from www.archaeopress.com

St Ninian and the Earliest Christianity in Scotland

Papers from the conference held by The Friends of the Whithorn Trust in Whithorn on September 15th 2007

Conference sponsored by Historic Scotland

Edited by Jane Murray

HISTORIC SCOTLAND

Contents

List of Contributors

Dave C Cowley, Royal Commission on the Ancient and Historic Monuments of Scotland

Katherine Forsyth, Department of Celtic, Glasgow University

Mike McCarthy, Department of Archaeological Sciences, University of Bradford

Ian Wood, School of History, University of Leeds

Jonathan Wooding, Department of Theology and Religious Studies, University of Wales Lampeter

Alex Woolf, Department of History, University of St Andrews

Foreword and acknowledgements

In 2007 the Friends of the Whithorn Trust celebrated twenty one years of the Trust's existence with a weekend event in place of the usual annual lecture. A full day conference was followed by an excursion to sites in the area. The conference, entitled 'St Ninian and the Earliest Christianity in Scotland', returned to the theme of the first Whithorn lecture given in 1992 by Charles Thomas, 'Whithorn's Christian Beginnings'. Professor Thomas had suggested that Bede's account of St Ninian's mission, encompassing his origins, the building of Candida Casa, establishment of a monastery, and the conversion of southern Scotland, might have 'flattened a three-century sequence into a single temporal plane'. He looked forward to publication of recent excavations at Whithorn to help to throw new light on this idea.

The excavation volume produced by Peter Hill in 1997 showed that the Glebe Field, adjacent to the site of the medieval cathedral, had been a settlement conurbation over an extended period stretching back to the fifth century. The nature of the earliest ecclesiastical activity on the summit of the hill remained, however, opaque, and speculation has continued over the existence of a Christian community here, and its relationship to St Ninian and his supposed mission to the Picts. With the added stimulus of Historic Scotland's re-presentation of the exhibition of carved stones in the Priory Museum in 2006, and with new work on the stones themselves, it was time to return to the theme of fifth century Whithorn.

The Friends of the Whithorn Trust would like to thank Historic Scotland for their sponsorship of this event. They are grateful to all the speakers who made the conference so absorbing and stimulating, to Professor Ted Cowan and Peter Hill who chaired the sessions, and to Peter Yeoman, who, with Adrian Cox, led a tour of the Priory Museum and the cathedral ruins. Visits to St Ninian's Chapel at the Isle of Whithorn and to St Ninian's Cave were rendered especially memorable by the wetness and wildness of the weather. As ever, the Friends owe a huge debt to Janet Butterworth, Business Manager of the Whithorn Trust, who ensured that everything ran smoothly.

In relation to the present volume, thanks are due to the speakers for producing texts for publication, only Catherine Swift being unable to contribute her interesting perspective based on the Irish experience of the ambiguous nature of fifth century conversion. Dave Cowley designed and realised the cover, with its aerial photograph of Whithorn in its landscape, and the superimposed Petrus Stone, which appears by courtesy of RCAHMS. Dave has also been a great help in preparing the illustrations.

Jane Murray

1. Introduction

Alex Woolf

In September 2007 the Friends of the Whithorn Trust decided to celebrate the twenty-first anniversary of the Trust. Instead of the usual annual lecture delivered on the Saturday evening closest to the Feast of St Ninian by an invited expert on a theme relating to Whithorn's history and archaeology, the decision was taken to hold a day conference in which a number of experts, each with their own specialism, would be invited to speak on the theme of St Ninian and the Earliest Christianity in Scotland. Six speakers were invited to address a mixed audience comprised of visiting academics and interested locals. This admixture of amateur and professional has been one of the hallmarks of the activities of the Friends over the years and has led to high quality research being presented with admirable clarity in past Lectures. The 2007 conference was no exception. The speakers were drawn from a range of disciplines and institutions. Wales and Ireland each provided a speaker, and Scotland and Yorkshire a pair each. Our Irish speaker, Dr Catherine Swift of the University of Limerick, was, due to pressing commitments, unable to provide us with a worked-up text of her paper for the present volume, but all the others have done so and these can be found in the pages that follow.

Dr Swift's paper dealt with the evidence provided by St Patrick's writings for what it must have been like to be a missionary operating beyond the Frontier in the last days of the Western Roman Empire. Christianity seems to have come to Whithorn at about the same time as Patrick laboured on the Irish mission field, and his career gives us a contemporary insight into the life of a Romano-British bishop beyond the *Limes*. The experiences of the earliest ecclesiastics at Whithorn must have been broadly comparable to that of Patrick and his followers in Ireland. The volume opens with a very useful and stimulating paper by Jonathan Wooding of the University of Wales Lampeter. Jonathan's connection to Whithorn goes back to his time as a student volunteer on Peter Hill's excavations in 1987, the very year the Friends were registered as a charity. His own intellectual and professional development has run in parallel to that of the site. In his paper he usefully reviews the way in which the scholarly expectation of an early 'Celtic' monastery has changed since archaeological investigations began at Whithorn, charting the way in which the image of a monastic missionary church established on beach heads by heroic figures has given way to a more organic expansion of Late Roman Christian structures within and beyond the former provinces of Britannia.

In some ways the theme of Christianity and the Roman Empire runs through most of the papers in this volume. Traditional views that there was sharp end to the Empire at Hadrian's Wall, and that 'Romanisation' is reflected in the archaeological traces we label 'Roman villas', have increasingly been called into question. Katherine Forsyth's paper focuses on a single monument, the Latinus stone. This is the oldest unambiguous evidence for Christianity at Whithorn, and perhaps in Scotland, dating, according to a comparative study of the letter forms, to the fifth century, and perhaps the first half of that century. The individual commemorated, Latinus, self-evidently bears a Latin name, yet he is no Continental missionary for he is descended from Barrauados, a man with an unambiguously Celtic name. At the same time, however, some of the 'errors' in the written Latin on the stone, we are told, reflect spoken Romance dialects rather than formal school room Latin. These traits, found widely in the analogous inscribed stones of Wales, point to the fact that Romanisation still held a tight grip on a significant portion of the population well beyond the so-called 'civil zone' of villas and market towns (roughly coextensive with south-east England) decades, perhaps even a century or more, after Britain slipped from imperial control. The spread of Roman ideology beyond the traditional frontier may also be reflected in the subject of Dave Cowley's paper. Over the past decades archaeologists working in eastern Scotland have uncovered a number of cemeteries, often containing long cists (stone-lined graves), and characterised by extended inhumations on a broadly east west alignment, and without grave goods. Radiocarbon (C^{14}) dating has finally settled the dispute over the dating of these cemeteries and they are now fairly firmly located in the period from the fourth to the eighth century. This fashion in funerary practice spread across much of the Roman World during the later empire and was certainly the custom adopted by Christians. The early church, however, did not attempt to exert direct control of burial, and the abandonment of these cemeteries around the eighth century probably reflects the period at which burial in the precinct of a church became normal for the laity. The map of excavated examples of such cemeteries is largely confined to eastern Scotland south of the Tay, although the burials excavated at Whithorn itself appear to represent examples of the type. What Dave shows in his paper is that aerial photography can reveal the presence of such cemeteries in the south-west as well, where the predominance of livestock farming over cereal production in the present is less conducive to traditional means of archaeological detection. The large size and location of some of these cemeteries suggests that, as elsewhere, they served large communities who lived and farmed in the surrounding landscape. As with the language inscribed upon the monument to Latinus, *nepos* of Barrouados, these cemeteries seem to reflect traditional communities adopting a Roman cultural package, quite possibly including Christianity, just as the empire begins to contract. Perhaps we should see the fourth to sixth centuries, so crucial for Whithorn's early development, as a period when the frontiers of the Roman Empire became more permeable, the holes that let the barbarians in also letting *romanitas* out.

Mike McCarthy, an old friend of Whithorn and former Chair of the Research Committee set up to advise the Friends, provides us with the evidence for Christianity in the northern part of the diocese of Britain in the later Roman period. In his paper Mike catalogues a range of categories of evidence, inscriptional, architectural and archaeological, which all suggest that the ruling class at least, in northern Britain, were to a large extent Christian and Christianised by the end of the fourth century. It is increasingly being recognised that despite the lack of impressive 'fabric', northern England contained a number of *ciuitas* capitals, the cities which formed the lynchpins of the Roman Empire, probably including, but not necessarily limited to, North Ferriby (Humberside), Aldburgh (Yorkshire), Corbridge (Northumberland) and Carlisle (Cumbria). Each of these would have had its own bishop and supporting clergy, and York, home to a provincial governor and a military *dux*, would have had a metropolitan bishop overseeing his colleagues. What also comes out in Mike's paper is the Cosmopolitan nature of northern society in this period, not just around the gubernatorial palace in York, but also on the frontier where we learn that a unit of bargees from Mesopotamia were employed on the Tyne, doubtless carrying goods and equipment between Corbridge and the North Sea ports. Not only did Christianity penetrate the province but there is also evidence suggesting a Jewish community on Tyneside.

The final paper of the day, and in this volume, was by Ian Wood, Professor of Medieval History at the University of Leeds and one of the World's leading experts on fifth- and sixth-century Gaul. Those interested in Whithorn and St Ninian cannot have failed to notice that of late there has been some controversy about the dates and identity of Saint Ninian himself. Medieval hagiographers presented him as a younger contemporary of Saint Martin of Tours (died 397), but recently a number of scholars, most notably Alan MacQuarrie and Thomas Clancy, have put forward serious arguments that a sixth-century date would make more sense. In his paper Ian Wood examines 'what difference' these two possibilities would make on the assumption that the basic narrative drawn from the saint's *dossier*, that he was a native Briton and visited Rome. An 'early' Ninian is compared to people like Faustus, bishop of Riez, a Briton who went to Provence to become a monk, Germanus of Auxerre, and Palladius, the papal missionary sent to Ireland in 431. A 'late' Ninian is compared to Samson of Dol, the Briton Winnoc encountered by Gregory of Tours, and the Irish monastic founder, Columbanus. The status of Rome, the cult of Saint Martin and the ease of travel between Britain and Gaul in the two periods is compared and contrasted, and the reader is encouraged to contextualise the two models for understanding Ninian's career and to evaluate how an earlier or later dating would affect our interpretation of the saint's role.

What all of the papers in this volume do is to contextualise the early history of Christian Whithorn firmly within the milieu of the later Roman Empire and the processes that are increasingly referred to by scholars as the 'Transformation of the Roman World' rather than the 'Fall of the Roman Empire'. Palladius, Patrick, Ninian and Uinniau all belong to a period which saw Roman and Romanised aristocrats carrying the values of the late Empire beyond the traditional frontiers protected from the barbarians amongst whom they worked, not by the might of the legions, but by the *lorica* of their faith.

References

Clancy, T O 2001 'The Real St. Ninian', *The Innes Review: The Journal of the Scottish Catholic Historical Association* 52, 1-28.
Macquarrie, A 1987 'The date of St Ninian's Mission: a reappraisal', *Records of the Scottish Church History Society* 23, 1-25.

2. St Ninian: Archaeology and the *Dossier* of the Saint

Jonathan M Wooding

We no longer speak of the formative period of the early medieval British church as an 'age of the saints'. Saints and their cult sites, nonetheless, remain important in our vision of early British history, as recent studies of St Ninian show.[1] Until fairly recent times the historical role of the saint in his earthly life would have been the main focus of scholarly attention. A 'British School' of hagiographical scholars, following the lead of Rice Rees (1836), tended to accept the essential historicity of the saints as they are depicted in the medieval *Vitae* and to see the deeds of the saints in these sources as reflective of the significance of these figures in their own lifetimes.[2] Such an acceptance is found as late as the 1960s in the works of scholars such as E G Bowen (1969) or Nora Chadwick (1963). More recently, the tendency has been to consider the *Vitae* as manifestations of the 'cults' of the saints, by which is meant the veneration and promotion of the saint as patron and intercessionary figure, often at some remove from his or her earthly career. Saints, it probably does not need to be said, were—and often are—perceived as having continuing agency after the end of their earthly lives. Texts recorded key facts concerning the saints and documented their deeds—including miracles, many of which were posthumous. The Bollandists term the collection of evidence for a saint's cult a *dossier*: a set of recorded details, which can include a feast day, a known resting-place, a distinct set of miracles.[3] A *dossier* is not a narrative record but a set of reference points, or 'co-ordinates'. The 'infrastructure' of veneration created a substantial material as well as literary footprint, one which is relevant to archaeology. Secular leaders invested in churches to ensure temporal influence and spiritual gain. Pilgrims visited the shrines of saints, generating wealth and industry for those shrines. What I want to consider here, in the light of recent historical discussion of the saint, is whether archaeology can provide some further co-ordinates for the cult of St Ninian at Whithorn.

My discussion will centre on the discoveries made at Whithorn in the period 1984-91. The essays in this collection commemorate two decades of the Whithorn Trust, which was founded to support that excavation. My reflection on the excavation is in part a personal one: in August 1987 a younger Jonathan Wooding arrived in Whithorn at the beginning of several seasons' work on the site. The 1984-91 excavation occurred in the middle of a period of revision of historical conceptions of the insular churches and of archaeological approaches to historic subjects. My experience of the excavation, and the Trust's engagement with the historical questions concerning Whithorn, was especially formative in my later career as a scholar of

---

[1] Most recently in Clancy 2001; 2002, 399-404; Fraser 2002; MacQueen 2005. A new interest in St Ninian was inspired by the excavation itself, including Peter Hill's own interest in St Ninian (Hill 1997, 14-16). See also Broun 1991; MacQueen 1991; Macquarrie 1987.

[2] This model was continued by John Fisher (1907) and Sabine Baring-Gould, as well inspiring Breton scholars such as Joseph Loth and René Largillière. See Davies 2002; Wooding 2007b.

[3] The Bollandists are the Belgian organisation responsible for the *Acta Sanctorum*. On the concept of a *dossier* made up of a number of 'co-ordinates' (*coordinèes*), see Delehaye 1934, 13. On genealogy as an additional co-ordinate in the Irish context, see Grosjean 1959, 389.

saints and the early church. I hope I can convey a little of the excitement of the experience in reflecting on what we have learnt from the discoveries of that time.

I

When the Glebe Field was investigated in 1984 Kathleen Hughes (1981) had already made a preliminary assault on the unitary model of the Celtic Church in her 1975 O'Donnell Lecture, published posthumously in 1981. Wendy Davies would complete the job (Davies 1992). Richard Sharpe's extensive critique of the 'monastic model' for the early Irish church had appeared in the 1984 volume of *Peritia* (Sharpe 1984), but its impact would take some time to be fully felt.[4] These studies brought a final end to the long-standing conception of the 'Celtic Church'. This model had been the product of a prior assumption that a relatively late acquisition of Christianity bestowed a particular character upon the Christianity of the Celtic world. It had two main premises. One was that the post-Roman church of the 'Celtic West' owed little, if anything, to survivals from the Christianity of the Roman period in Britain. The second was that this late, possibly eccentric, development of the church led to an unconventional model of pastoral care, dominated by monastic organisation and possibly inherited from a wholesale transplantation of monks from Gaul. Neither of these premises is now sustainable. Since the 1950s, archaeological evidence has shown that Christianity in Roman Britain was established over a much wider area than had been suggested by the limited documentary sources (Petts 2003, 19-23). Historical studies since the 1980s have identified the role of the bishop in early Ireland and Wales as not differing in its fundamentals from that elsewhere in western Europe— especially Anglo-Saxon England (Etchingham 1999, esp 172-238; Blair 2005, 73-8). Monasticism was a major force in church organisation, but the 'Celtic Church' of late foundation, in which bishops played a negligible role, is an historiographical myth.

We need not dwell on the causes of the earlier conception. Twenty years ago it was still one of a number of possible models which informed our reading of Whithorn. Were we looking for a Roman period foundation, one from the 'age of the saints', or something more recent? Was Ninian a late-Roman bishop, ministering to an established Christian community, a travelling monastic founder making a missionary 'bridgehead', or was he simply a concoction of posthumous hagiography? The pull of the 'British School' was still considerable. E G Bowen's 'Dad's Army' style maps, with arrows showing the travels of saints, seductively drew medieval pilgrim chapels into narratives in which they became missionary 'bridgeheads' (Wooding 2007a). The 'British School' had a Scottish disciple in Douglas Simpson for whom Ninian was a 'Celtic' saint, and 'Celtic' saints lived by the shore, hence his argument in 1940 had been that the chapel at the Isle of Whithorn was the logical place to seek *Candida Casa*, rather than the medieval Whithorn Priory (Simpson 1940, 75-6). To an extent the excavations at Whithorn were a test of the new, revisionist interpretation which might seek an early episcopal seat in an inland centre. It was right to remain open-minded, and in 2007 we would be more confident in ruling out the older model than we were in 1987.

The opportunity to test older assumptions was therefore one reason why Whithorn was an exciting place twenty years ago. Another was that an overlap of historical and archaeological questions was fairly rare in excavations of the 1980s. Sites datable to AD 400-800 were mostly identified on the basis of finds of imported pottery: red slip-wares and amphorae of Mediterranean origin (ARS, PRS, B ware), and coarseware of Gaulish origin (E ware). One of the most notable characteristics of these types at the time was their general confinement to sites which were ahistorical, or at best para-historical. Finds had been made at sites such as Tintagel, South Cadbury, Congresbury, Garranes, Longbury Bank, Dinas Powys—all major early medieval sites, but only arguably 'historic', if at all (for discussion, see Campbell 2007, 14-26; Wooding 1996, 41-54). At Whithorn in 1984 substantial finds of early pottery occurred at a site

---

[4] Though dated 1984, Sharpe's article did not make a major impact on scholarship until late in the decade; Sharpe's revisionist model has also partly made its mark through the advocacy of Colmán Etchingham, eg 1991; 1999.

with a complex documentary record.[5] I recall my sense of satisfaction on reading the first reports of the 1984 finds that this had finally occurred.

In the interim, archaeology and history had somewhat gone their separate ways. In 1977 David Dumville had published his now notorious review of two books, one by John Morris (*The Age of Arthur*) and the other by Leslie Alcock (*Arthur's Britain*) (Dumville 1977). Leslie, of course, as a member of research committee made a major contribution to the Whithorn Trust in its first years.[6] Yet in 1987 he was a much-criticised figure for his interest in historical archaeology. One thing that may not be remembered now is how much a generation of archaeologists drew inspiration from Dumville's assault on the historical element of the Alcock's book. Medieval archaeologists of the 'New Archaeology' school, most notably Philip Rahtz, were at the time promoting the idea that there could be a 'text-free' interpretation of the material record. For them Dumville's position seemed supportive.[7] In prehistoric studies such positions had already been adopted in reaction to the priorities of an older generation that was perceived as preoccupied with military structures and invasions, inclined to cast hundreds of years of prehistory in the light of Roman accounts of the conquest of late-Iron Age Europe (Cunliffe 1974, 345-7; 1976; Clark 1966). Early historic studies were not entirely comparable to the prehistoric case, inasmuch as the documentary record, such as it is, covers a longer proportion of the early historic period. There had been legitimate concerns, however, about the influence of the Arthurian legend upon the interpretation of south-western sites, notably on Leslie Alcock's own excavation at South Cadbury.[8] Yet in 1987 there were many, myself amongst them, who could only see these ideas of separation of archaeological and historical interpretation as a stage along the way to forming a more critical basis for the encounter between history and archaeology; which was, anyway, more or less untested by a serious collision of a well-documented site with major archaeological discoveries. A number of us also saw the very thoughtful archaeological synthesis of Alcock's book as an unfortunate casualty of attacks upon its weak historical preamble. History is arguably not only about texts, but Celtic historiography, at least at the moment, appears wary of venturing much beyond them.[9] Certainly there are serious problems if we start to pursue archaeology in thrall to history, but archaeology can certainly bear weight upon historical judgement, especially as we move outside the sphere of narrative sources—often the case with the earliest historic period. It is also arguable that archaeology which is cast purely in ahistoric language can be unnecessarily dull reading (eg Burrow 1981; Reece 1981). We were not 'digging up St Ninian' twenty years ago, but what we found was potentially, if not certainly, related to his cult. Can we find a language to interpret these data in historical analysis at Whithorn?

II

The finds at Whithorn in 1984, from five trenches in the Glebe Field, were a bit of a surprise. The field had already been tested in 1972 by Christopher Tabraham, albeit under very trying conditions, and though this testing turned up suggestive evidence it did not produce any early artefacts (Tabraham 1979). What was immediately striking from the 1984 excavation was the

---

[5] There had been earlier finds from Iona and Clogher, both historic sites, and an at that time unnoticed find from Caldey.

[6] It is right here also to record my debt to Leslie's encouragement, including his recommendation that I join the Whithorn excavation.

[7] On New Archaeology in general, see Clarke 1973; on 'New Medieval Archaeology', see Rahtz 1981. My perspective on these debates is also based on conversations I had during 1987 with a number of the protagonists.

[8] For criticism, see Thomas 1969, and replies. For the interpretation of South Cadbury in terms of an 'Arthur-type' figure, see Alcock 1972. Lying behind much of the criticism of Alcock was a longer history of criticism centring on Sir Mortimer Wheeler, both for his use of 'Arthur' to raise the profile of excavations (his own at Caerleon, and as chair of research committee at South Cadbury), and for his historicist interpretation of Iron Age sites. See Hawkes 1982, 96-8, 172, 176, 342-30.

[9] For two comments on Celtic historiography that reflect on the centrality of the text and its distance from traditional historiography, see Davies 1983, 67; Byrne 1971, 2. Byrne's remarks on the need to keep *both* philology and archaeology separate from the historian's task are also thoughtful, (*ibid*, 9).

chronological range of the finds and their variety of ethnic associations: Mediterranean, Gaulish, Anglo-Saxon, Hiberno-Norse, as well as local (Hill 1985).

The 'rescue' ideology of the 1970s had been somewhat against large research excavations. This ideology was still at work in the early '80s, yet there was a recognition that the type of understanding gained by studying successive phases, the chronological relationships between them, and the extent of the area of the different phases, was more meaningful for the understanding of the past.[10] This was better accomplished by large, open area, excavation. Such study of a site can consider questions which are central to both history and archaeology. When did the site commence? When did it achieve its greatest extent? What were the factors that made it grow and diminish? When change occurred to the layout of the site, what does this change tell us about the ethos—in which you may include spirituality or charism if you want—of the new and the old regime? We are looking to study the life of the people on the site and we are looking to identify the events which occurred that had major impacts upon the continuity of that life. The 1986 decision to found the Whithorn Trust and pursue these questions through a major research excavation was important for our understanding of church history as well as archaeology.

The 1984 finds, and the first of 1986, all showed that the Northumbrian presence at Whithorn was substantial, exactly as one would infer from Bede's *Historia Ecclesiastica* (III § 4). The 1984 finds also indicated a more or less constant use of the site back to the time of the Mediterranean imports (ARS, PRS, B ware). In other words, they made more likely that the Northumbrian cult of St Ninian had its roots in a genuine continuity of Christianity on the site from at least c500. Such could have been argued from the Latinus Stone, perhaps, but the evidence of a continuous development of the site across the intervening period was new data.[11]

The retreat from the belief in the heroic deeds of the saint as simply recorded in *Vitae* has led to a tendency to pull the development of the cult of the saint to a point after his or her own lifetime. The cult is understood as not necessarily deriving its importance from the actual deeds or personality of the saint him- or herself and not necessarily from the site of his or her original activity. If a relic, for example, were brought to a site, a cult might be built around that relic unrelated to where the saint lived out his life. In the model propounded by Pádraig Ó Riain for the earliest Irish saints, the period between the *floruit* of many monastic founders and the horizon of surviving texts may been one in which the co-ordinates of the saints were poorly recorded and subject to conflation of figures and even manipulation of data.[12] Ó Riain's model has been applied to Whithorn by Thomas Clancy, who argues that Ninian is only a doublet of St Finnian—also Ó Riain's primary case-study in Ireland—a British saint active in Ireland.[13] In this model, Finnian's cult may have formed elsewhere, been brought to Whithorn and, through misreading of the name, become that of a separate figure—or Whithorn may have been 'Finnian's' primary site (Clancy 2001).[14]

The continuity and extent of settlement on a cult site may play a part in testing the reasonableness of a hypothesis such as Clancy's. As James Fraser has indicated, a key weakness of Clancy's argument is in its assumption that the 'literary cult' of Ninian can be presumed to

---

[10] It is worth noting that these perspectives evolved in odd ways. Wheeler was criticised in the 1930s for excavating too *little* of sites and of being only interested in military questions. In the 1960s and '70s the ideology was evolving that there was too *much* excavation of sites not under immediate threat. Much of this was about politics: the progressives of the '30s were in favour of understanding society, those of the '70s in favour of conservation. Both were arguably dialectical positions against the prevailing authority. For a summary, see Hawkes 1982, 176.

[11] This is more than archaeology telling us what we already know. A comparison can be made with the famous Pirenne thesis of continuous trade between the Eastern and Western Mediterranean in the fifth through to the eighth century. Historical sources showed that there were links in the fourth and the sixth centuries, but archaeology showed that there was hiatus in the fifth and seventh, either side of Justinian's reconquest. Material evidence in this way can show continuity or discontinuity in ways texts may not.

[12] For representative studies of his position, see Ó Riain 1982; 1997.

[13] I note Ó Riain's view differs from this in making Finnian Irish.

[14] On the wider identity of Finnian, see Dumville 1997; Ó Riain 1999.

have operated without reference to the cult site. If the name transmitted by Bede is misspelled, the fact that *two* sources possibly emanating from in Whithorn in the eighth century, Bede's own source and the *Miracula* of St Ninian, both use the form *Nyn-* and not *Uin-* is hard to explain: '… anyone based at Whithorn itself, or Galloway generally, will have been entirely aware that Uinniau, and not "Nyniau" was the name of the saint whose shrine at Whithorn continued to be the object of pilgrimage' (Fraser 2002, 54). Fraser adduces this as a reason why the *Miracula* was not composed at Whithorn, but the more obvious inference is that his prior assumption that one '*Uinniau*' was the real dedicatee, based on Clancy's hypothesis, is incorrect.[15]

I have not the time to do full justice to Clancy's important study, which raises important questions about the cult of Finnian in Scotland and its relationship to Ninian (Clancy 2001). As in the case of Ó Riain's hypothesis concerning Irish saints, the case of Finnian raises questions we need to answer carefully. I acknowledge also that constant repetition of the claim does not prove that the extant *Miracula* is unquestionably a Whithorn product, nor that Pecthelm, the first Anglo-Saxon abbot, is necessarily Bede's source. My concern here is to consider only the probability that the name *Uinniau* became, erroneously, 'Nynia' during the Northumbrian period at Whithorn. If we could show a distinct hiatus at Whithorn between the time of the Latinus stone (fifth/sixth century) and the time of Bede's informant this might support the assumption that the name was forgotten and incorrectly recovered from external sources. In fact what we can demonstrate is continuity. Most striking in the sequence is the fact that Pecthelm's monastery of the early 700s, which involved substantial reshaping of the site in the seventh and eighth centuries, stands in a direct relationship with the settlement that preceded it.

The 1986-91 excavation in the Southern Sector of the Glebe Field revealed a continuously waterlogged area which allowed preservation of dendro-chronological dates for posts from buildings in the sixth and through the seventh century. The dates leave little doubt as to continuity. Building I/24, not aligned to the later Northumbrian site grid and therefore continuous of the older settlement, produced dates ranged from AD 623, 630, 636, 681, 706. These can only be *terminus post quem* dates on account of the loss of outer rings: the extant outer ring is the earliest date the tree can have been felled, but such trimming rarely takes one back too far from the felling date (Hill 1997, 596).[16] The dates span the E ware horizon into the Northumbrian era and almost certainly show the continuous existence of this structure up to and beyond the Northumbrian takeover in c620-710. The fact that buildings survive up to the takeover must be held to prove that the Northumbrian takeover of Whithorn was of an established site. The site the Northumbrians took over around AD 700-730 was also of considerable extent. The Southern Sector excavation is at a distance of 70 metres from the presumed site nucleus, marked by the medieval priory.[17] The waterlogging of this sector suggests that by the seventh century space around the shrine was also at a premium.

The fact that the settlement seems to have neither contracted nor been abandoned just prior to the Northumbrian takeover makes it hard to argue that the Northumbrians did anything more than put their stamp on a going concern (Pollock 1992, 109, 141-2). The fact that the 'stamp' put upon the site was such a major realignment can be read as a response to the scale of the challenge to make their mark. This is appropriation rather than the 'manufacture' of history—a crucial distinction.

---

[15] I would agree with Geoffrey Barrow that a later, rather than earlier, conflation with Finnian is sufficient to explain the problems raised by Thomas Clancy (Barrow 2004, 8-10).

[16] For the history of this building, see Hill 1997, 132-3, 140.

[17] The subsequent excavations in 1992 showed a similar extent to the site on the northern side (Pollock 1992).

III

One of the most interesting comparisons brought to my attention while I was at Whithorn was between Whithorn and St Davids (Pembrokeshire), a site most recently of interest to me. Peter Hill observed that the two sites resembled each other in their central location of a major church in the centre of a peninsula, Dewisland, and with chapel sites at various points on the coast around it (James 1993). I could add to this the fact, also noted to me by Peter Hill, that the church at Whithorn is almost invisible as one approaches from most directions.[18] This is also the case at St Davids, where the cathedral is rather unexpectedly located at the bottom of a valley. There are also comparable historiographical debates. A received tradition at St Davids is that the early church of St David was not at the present, inland, site. One interpretation would have David's cult moved posthumously to St Davids from a monastery in Ceredigion (Evans 2007, 38-40). Another claims that it was in Dewisland, but was likely to have been a coastal 'bridgehead' at Whitesands Bay (Wooding 2007a, 218; Badger and Green 1925). This compares to the claims made by Simpson for the Isle of Whithorn.

It is worth remembering here that the ideas of Rice Rees and his subsequent school have their roots in medieval legends of sea-driven saints, which themselves interpret the dedications and sites in the landscape into seductive narratives (Wooding 2007a, 214-20). Clancy (2001, 1) rightly observes with respect to Whithorn that often 'we allow late narrative evidence to dictate the agenda for a period whose best remains are non-narrative in form'. The same governing principles are at work here. The holy man in search of a 'desert' would live on the coast, either because of the hostility of a pagan inland and/or because he arrived from the sea. The site suitable for a monastery might not be suitable for a cathedral. The common factor to all such theories is that they flourish in a vacuum of early evidence and hinge on philological ambiguities of names that can be identified with more than one site. Medieval writers sketched narratives from such evidence that cloud our reading of the earlier periods.

Can we get back beyond these narratives? In the light of my foregoing discussion it is a particular irony that a recent defence of the views of John Morris, by of all people, David Dumville, should draw attention to the fact that our present lack of early sources does not necessarily reflect the reality of first millennium life at St Davids. Dumville has reasserted a point made long ago by Morris that the account of the rule of St David's community which is included in the *Vita S Dauid* by Rhygyfarch ap Sulien (d 1099) is almost certainly based on an early text preserved by the church of Menevia (St Davids) from the sixth into the eleventh century (Dumville 2001; Morris 1966, 349-50, 384-5). The correspondences between Rhygyfarch's account and the *ca* sixth-century *Fragmenta* of Gildas—a letter to Finnian, whether in Ireland or at Whithorn!—strongly suggest that Rhygyfarch was using a genuinely early source (Winterbottom (ed) 1980, 143-5, and notes 154-5).[19] As Rhygyfarch was the son of a bishop of Menevia it is perfectly natural he would have access to such early sources which survived up until the middle ages, but have not survived to this day. In Rhygyfarch's words, '... eaten away along the edges and the spines by the constant devouring of grubs and the ravages of the passing years, and written in the handwriting of our forefathers, they have survived until now'.[20] One of the features of Rhygyfarch's *Vita*, as I have argued elsewhere, is that it takes in what are clearly challenging co-ordinates for St David. David was an extremely ascetic figure, his theology was hardly that of an eleventh-century bishop. Rhygyfarch works hard to harmonise these aspects with the requirements of an eleventh-century Welsh audience seeking an archiepiscopal saint to oppose Norman claims. That he needs to work hard to do so indicates that he was not able to simply 're-invent' the saint—any more than subsequent generations were simply able to move David's major church from the remote, wet, valley of St Davids, more

---

[18] Peter Hill, I note, adduces the hidden character of Whithorn *proper* as a suitable attribute not simply for a monastic site, but a missionary site of Gauls, a further elaboration on the bridgehead theory (Hill 2001, 26).

[19] The citation of Gildas by Columbanus confirms the early date of Gildas's text.

[20] '... *uetustissimis patriae,maxime ipsius ciuitatis ... quae assidua tinearum edacitate ac annosis aeui terebraminibus per oras et cardines corrosa, ac ex antiquo seniorum stilo conscripta, nunc usque supersunt*', *Vita S Dauid* § 66, ed and transl Sharpe, R & Davies, J R 2007; Wooding 2007b, 15-18.

appropriate to an ascetic than an episcopal life, to a more easily accessible location (Williams 2007, 335-7). Not only he, but his local audience knew the co-ordinates of the early cult of David.

IV

The case of St Davids emphasises the importance of factoring continuity into our judgement. At St Davids we have no early archaeological evidence. At Whithorn we have no literary evidence to take us with certainty back beyond the Northumbrian horizon, but as we have seen with the case of St David the likelihood of continuity of records at a site can be established. At Whithorn, the fact of continuity across the crucial phase at the end of the seventh century makes more likely a comparable continuity of records, as well as emphasising that, whatever was the dominant cult at Whithorn up to that time, it had a substantial material footprint.

I have said less about the period before the seventh century, the time of St Ninian himself. Did the excavations of 1984-91 tell us more about this figure? At the time we were inclined to say that the 'new' discovery of the excavation was the extent of the Northumbrian presence and its realignment of the site. I have noted, however, that in some ways the importance of the excavation was to show the scale of the site prior to the Northumbrian takeover. The eighth-century cult is thus only the reshaping of a site which had been long in the making. What light can we also shed on the transition from the 'real' Ninian to the period of the cult?

The Whithorn excavation turned up datable material stretching as far back as cAD 500. This was not entirely unexpected, as the Latinus stone is of this general date (Thomas 1992, 1-10). What was not found was material evidence of an earlier date. The failure to extend the chronology back beyond c500 was important in Alan Macquarrie's hypothesis that Whithorn was a '… "greenfield" site colonised by incomers c500' (Macquarrie 1997, 51, 53 — a revision of Macquarrie 1987). The historical case Macquarrie sets out focuses on the limited value of the pillars of an early fifth-century date and in particular the medieval synchronism of Ninian with Martin of Tours (Sharpe 2002, 109). When we turn to the evidence of Bede, he only says that Ninian worked *multo ante tempore* with respect to St Columba (arrived 563). How long is a 'long time' is debatable (MacQueen 2005, 22-4). One can agree with Macquarrie that Bede probably had little precise evidence on the matter—but a vested interest in having Ninian trump St Columba in preaching to the Picts. However, the archaeological evidence cannot really be a premise for Macquarrie's argument. Absence of evidence, as the saying goes, is not evidence of absence. The excavators struggled to take the occupation with certainty earlier than the contexts in which the Mediterranean wares were found, but this is a circular matter, as the AD 500 horizon derives primarily from the certainty provided by the Mediterranean imports, in the words of Charles Thomas 'often—too often—picked out by archaeologists as chronological life-rafts in an ocean of uncertainties' (Thomas 1976, 245). Even these, at their maximal dating bracket, could anyway take us back into the fifth century, with Campbell proposing phases of c475-525 and 525-550 (Campbell 2007, 26). Some dendro-chronological dates from the Southern Sector also give pause to any claim of a 'greenfield'. A plank (No. 8739) from a pit in the southern sector gave a *terminus post quem* of AD 466 (Hill 1997, 596; for context, see 173). Trimming of wood allows that this is not proof of a fifth-century date, but one would be unwilling to rule out earlier occupation, as indeed was the excavator (*ibid*, 69). A second point relates to distribution. The dendro-chronological material all comes from the Southern Sector, which is the furthest from the medieval priory and arguably from the nucleus of the original site. Biv and Bv amphora sherds come from the maximal extent of this sector. I would have my doubts as to Hill's model of importation of these alongside E ware (*ibid*, 324), but the distributions put putatively sixth-century material over the furthest extent of a site of considerable size. A shrine of a saint rarely emerges overnight. Both Hill and Macquarrie lean towards a model of a community arriving *en masse* and developing the site. However this, and Hill's speculations on Gaulish monks, following Charles Thomas, seem like echoes of the 'Celtic Church' model (*ibid*, 12; see Sharpe 2002, 95). If we allow for a longer period of evolution for a site of the size Whithorn appears to have been c500-550, the late fifth century may be too late to account for this. Hill rightly notes that on the area excavated and the evidence found there is every possibility that this was the expansion of an existing centre (*ibid*, 8). There is at the moment little to prevent this hypothetical nucleus of the site having been a settlement and shrine of the early fifth century, however much more likely the later date seems. The recent trend of text-criticism in Celtic Studies has been to pull dates forward in time. This need not, however, be grounds to assume early dates are always less plausible than later ones.

A second observation is that the retreat from credulous belief in the histories of early saints must also be balanced with the consciousness that Christianity in Britain stretches back beyond the 'age of the saints' into the late-Roman period—a point on which Charles Thomas, for example, seems sometimes ambiguous.[21] That the literary *dossier* depicts Ninian as a bishop 'regularly' educated is not incompatible with a fifth-century figure—unless we are to also place Patrick in the sixth century—indeed we know too little about the arrival of monasticism in Britain to make such assumptions.[22]

The site of Whithorn flourished in the early sixth century and flourished continuously beyond the Northumbrian takeover. This may be said to be a material aspect of the *dossier* of St Ninian—a non-narrative source—affirming the power and continuity of the site of his church from an early date. Peter Hill would speculate on some further elements which are consistently evinced in the record: white plaster, in keeping with the saint's literary associations; the detritus of a healing cult (Hill 1997, 19-20, 468-74). Certainly the idea of the 'white house', whether or not the original meaning of *candida casa*, became a material co-ordinate of the cult. Archaeology cannot put a name to the patron, but the burden of proof, in view of the continuity of the settlement, is surely on those who would argue that it was not 'Ninian' from the beginning.

I hope these brief, at times personal, reflections on Whithorn '84-91' provide some insight into what a scholar of early British saints and churches found inspirational about Whithorn. Great excavations only come along now and again and they tend to be formative of generations of scholars. Whithorn was certainly one of those.

References

Alcock, L 1972 'By South Cadbury that is Camelot ...'. London.

Badger, A R & Green, F 1925 'The chapel traditionally attributed to St Patrick, Whitesand Bay, Pembrokeshire', Archaeologia Cambrensis 80, 87-120.

Barrow, G W S 2004 Saint Ninian and Pictomania (The Twelfth Whithorn Lecture 2003). Friends of the Whithorn Trust, Whithorn.

Blair, J 2005 The Church in Anglo-Saxon Society. Oxford.

Bowen, E G 1969 Saints, Seaways and Settlements in the Celtic Lands. Cardiff.

Broun, D 1991 'The literary record of St Nynia: fact and fiction', Innes Review 42, 143-50.

Burrow, I 1981 *Hillforts and Hilltop Settlement in Somerset*. Oxford (=Brit Archaeol Rep, Brit Ser 90).

Byrne, F J 1971 'Ireland before the Norman invasion', *in* Moody, T W (ed) *Irish History 1945-70,* 1-15. Dublin.

Campbell, E 2007 Continental and Mediterranean Imports to Atlantic Britain and Ireland, AD 400-800 (=CBA Research Report 157), 14-26. York.

Chadwick, N 1963 *The Age of Saints in the Celtic Church.* Oxford.

Clancy, T O 2001 'The real St Ninian', *Innes Review* 52 , 1-28.

---

[21] For a recent summary, see Sharpe 2002, 94-105; on Thomas, *ibid*, 95.
[22] On Patrick and monasticism, see Herren 1989, 76-85.

Clancy, T O 2002 'Scottish Saints and national identities in the Middle Ages', *in* Thacker & Sharpe (eds), 397-422.

Clark, G 1966 'The invasion hypothesis in British archaeology', *Antiquity* 40, 172-89.

Clarke, D 1973 'Archaeology: The loss of innocence', *Antiquity* 47, 6-18.

Cunliffe, B 1974 *The Iron Age Communities of Britain*, 2nd ed. London.

Cunliffe, B 1976 'The Iron Age', *in* Renfrew, C (ed) *British Prehistory: a New Outline*, 233-62. London.

Davies, J R 2002 'The Saints of south Wales and the Welsh Church' *in* Thacker & Sharpe (eds), 361-95.

Davies, W 1983 'An historian's view of Celtic archaeology', *in* Hinton, D (ed) *25 Years of Medieval Archaeology*, 67-73. Sheffield.

Davies, W 1992 'The myth of the Celtic Church', *in* Edwards, N & Lane, A (eds) *The Early Church in Wales and the West*), 12-21. Oxford.

Delehaye, H 1934 *Cinq leçons sur la méthode hagiographique*. Brussels.

Dumville, D N 1977 'Sub-Roman Britain—history and legend', *History* 62, 173-92.

Dumville, D N 1997 'Finnian of Movilla: Briton, Gael, Ghost?' *in* Proudfoot, L (ed) *Down: History and Society*, 71-84. Dublin.

Dumville, D N 2001 *Saint David of Wales* (=Kathleen Hughes Memorial Lectures on Mediaeval Welsh History 1). Cambridge.

Etchingham, C 1991 'The Early Irish Church: Some observations on pastoral care and dues', *Ériu* 42, 99-118.

Etchingham, C 1999 *Church Organisation in Ireland, AD 650 to 1000*. Naas.

Evans, J W 2007 'Transition and survival: St David and St Davids Cathedral', *in* Evans & Wooding (eds), 20-40.

Evans, J W & Wooding, J M (eds) 2007 *St David of Wales—Cult, Church and Nation*, Studies in Celtic History 24. Woodbridge.

Fisher, J 1907 'Welsh church dedications, *Trans of the Honourable Society of Cymmrodorion* (1906-7), 76-108.

Fraser, J 2002 'Northumbrian Whithorn and the making of St Ninian', *The Innes Review* 53, 40-59.

Grosjean, P 1959 'Déchiffrement d'un groupe de *Notulae* du Livre d'Armagh sur S. Patrice (numéros 28-41)', *Analecta Bollandiana* 77, 387-411.

Hawkes, J 1982 *Mortimer Wheeler*. London.

Herren, M 1989 'Mission and monasticism in the *Confessio* of St. Patrick' *in* Corráin, D Ó, Breatnach, L, & McCone, K (eds) *Sages, Saints and Storytellers*, 76-85. Maynooth.

Hill, P 1985 'Whithorn', *Current Archaeology* 96, 27-9.

Hill, P 1997 *Whithorn and St Ninian: The Excavation of a Monastic Town 1984-91*, Sutton/Whithorn Trust, Stroud.

Hill, P 2001 'Whithorn, Latinus and the origins of Christianity', *in* Hamerow, H & MacGregor, A (eds) *Image and Power in the Archaeology of Early Medieval Britain: essays in honour of Rosemary Cramp*, 23-32. Oxbow Books, Oxford.

Hughes, K 1981 'The Celtic Church: is this a valid concept?', *Cambridge Medieval Celtic Studies* 1, 1-20.

James, H 1993 'The cult of St David in the Middle Ages', *in* Carver, M (ed) *In Search of Cult: Archaeological Investigations in honour of Philip Rahtz*, 105-11. Woodbridge. Also *J Pembrokeshire Historical Soc* 7 (1996-7) 5-25.

Macquarrie, A 1987 'The date of St Ninian's Mission: a reappraisal', *Records of the Scottish Church History Society* 23, 1-25.

Macquarrie, A 1997 'St Ninian of Whithorn', *in* Macquarrie, A *The Saints of Scotland*, 50-73. Edinburgh.

MacQueen, J 1991 'The literary sources for the Life of St Ninian', *in* Oram, R & Stell, G (eds) *Galloway: Land and Lordship*, 17-25. Edinburgh.

MacQueen, J 2005 *St Nynia* (3rd ed). Edinburgh.

Morris, J 1966 'The dates of the Celtic Saints', *J of Theological Studies* 17, 342-91.

Ó Riain, P 1978 '*The Making of a Saint: Finbarr of Cork 600-1200*. London.

Ó Riain, P 1982 'Towards a Methodology in Early Irish Hagiography', *Peritia* 1, 146-60.

Ó Riain, P 1999 'Finnio and Winniau: a return to the subject' *in* Carey, J, Koch, J, & Lambert, P-Y (eds) *Ildánach Ildírech—a Festschrift for Proinsias Mac Cana*, 187-202. Andover MA and Aberystwyth.

Petts, P 2003 *Christianity in Roman Britain*. Tempus, Stroud.

Pollock, D 1992 *Whithorn* 5 (=Interim Report). Whithorn.

Rahtz, P 1981 *The New Medieval Archaeology*. York.

Reece, R 1981 *Excavations in Iona 1964 to 1974*. London.

Rees, R 1836 *Essay on the Welsh Saints or the Primitive Christians usually considered to be the founders of churches in Wales*. London.

Sharpe, R 1984 'Some problems concerning the organisation of the Church in Early Medieval Ireland', *Peritia* 3, 230-70.

Sharpe, R 2002 'Martyrs and local Saints in Late Antique Britain', *in* Thacker & Sharpe (eds), 75-154.

Sharpe, R & Davies, J R 2007 *Vita S Dauid* in Evans & Wooding (eds), 152-3.

Simpson, W D 1940 *St Ninian and Christian origins in Scotland*. Edinburgh.

Tabraham, C 1979 'Excavations at *Whithorn* Priory, Wigtown District 1972 and 1975', *Trans Dumfriesshire Galloway Nat Hist Archaeol Soc* 3rd ser 54, 29-38.

Thacker, A and Sharpe, R (eds) 2002 *Local Saints and Local Cults in the Early Medieval* West. Oxford.

Thomas, C 1969 'Are These the Walls of Camelot?', *Antiquity* 43, 27-30.

Thomas, C 1976 'Imported post-Roman Mediterranean pottery in Ireland and western Britain, chronologies and implications', *Proc Royal Irish Academy* 76C, 245-55.

Thomas, C 1992 Whithorn's Christian beginnings (The First Whithorn Lecture). Friends of the Whithorn Trust, Whithorn.

Williams, G 2007 'The crisis of the sixteenth century', *in* Evans & Wooding (eds), 330-8.

Winterbottom, M (ed) 1980 *Gildas, The Ruin of Britain and Other Documents*. Chichester.

Wooding, J M 1996 *Communication and Commerce along the Western Sealanes AD 400-800*. Oxford. (=Brit Archaeol Rep, Internat Ser 654).

Wooding, J M 2007a 'Island and Coastal Churches and in Medieval Wales and Ireland', *in* Jankulak, K & Wooding, J M (eds) *Ireland and Wales in the Middle Ages*, 201-28. Dublin.

Wooding, J M 2007b 'The figure of David' *in* Evans & Wooding (eds), 1-19.

3. The Latinus Stone: Whithorn's Earliest Christian Monument

Katherine Forsyth

The inscribed stone memorial to Latinus and his unnamed daughter is Whithorn's—and Scotland's—earliest Christian monument. Although simple and visually unassuming it is an object which repays close scrutiny for it has much to tell us about the origins of Whithorn and the origins of Christianity in Scotland. The earliest phases of Whithorn's history are poorly understood and the Latinus Stone itself is a lone witness to the site's fifth-century origin. What follows is a detailed investigation of the monument and its inscription in the context of contemporary epigraphic practice elsewhere in Western Britain. I have adopted Nash-William's label 'Group 1' to apply to these British Latin inscriptions, some of them Latin/ogham bi-lingual, which range in date from the fifth to the early seventh century (Nash-Williams 1950). It is hoped that a better understanding of the social and archaeological context of these kindred monuments will clarify the significance of the Latinus stone and provide important clues as to the likely nature of the Whithorn site and its inhabitants in the fifth century.

Note: Following Sims-Williams 2003, 'Group 1' inscribed monuments are identified by their number in CIIC (Macalister 1945, 1949) followed by an oblique line and their number in the relevant regional corpus: Nash-Williams 1950 (for Wales), Okasha 1993 (for Devon and Cornwall) and Kermode 1907 (for Man). References for all 'Group 1' inscriptions mentioned are given in the appendix. Roman inscriptions are identified by their number in the corpus RIB (Collingwood and Wright 1965).

Provenance

The 'Latinus' stone was discovered in 1890[1] during William Galloway's excavation of Whithorn Priory. Galloway died in 1897 before he could publish the results of his excavation, and so the details of the stone's discovery must be pieced together from various, occasionally contradictory, sources. The most reliable account appears to be that of P M'Kerlie who states that the stone was discovered 'when the gravelled walk in front of the parish church was opened up […] lying close behind the north wall of the old cathedral (P M'Kerlie 1906, 435; see also E M'Kerlie 1916, 83).[2] It has been suggested that the exact location of this discovery is indicated on Galloway's plan of the Priory (Hill 1997), however, the subsequent discovery of unpublished correspondence from Galloway to the Marquis of Bute clarifies the plan. It is now clear that neither the 'frag of cross' nor the 'pillar' marked on it are the Latinus stone (Watt 2001, 137-9).[3]

---

[1] Craig discusses the evidence for this date in detail (1997, 614) and refutes Allen's statement (Allen & Anderson 1903, 496-7) that it was found in 1891.

[2] Radford's assertion that the Latinus stone was found at the east end of church (1956, 171)—in which he was followed by Thomas (1992a, 1992b, etc.)—has been shown by Craig to be erroneous (for a detailed discussion of the evidence of the stone's discovery, including unpublished archival material, see Craig 1997, 614-6; 1992, 285-9).

[3] Rather, they are, respectively, WHP.EC.19 and a later medieval column-base.

We are left with M'Kerlie's general description of the find-spot which, in any case, is almost certainly a secondary context.

It is becoming clear that virtually all the Early Medieval sculpture from Whithorn has survived because it was built into the walls of the Medieval priory. Many pieces bear clear signs of having been cut down for use as building blocks (most strikingly: WHP.EC.10, EC.30, EC.19, EC.17).[4] Some were even found *in situ* in later Medieval walls (for instance three pieces found in the 1960s during Roy Ritchie's excavation: EC.37 built into the north-east corner of the nave, and EC. 36 and EC.38 found in the north side of the crypt (Lowe forthcoming). It is likely that the Latinus stone was preserved in the same manner. The re-used Early Medieval blocks represent only a tiny proportion of the total masonry of the Priory and cannot have been needed because of a shortage of quarried stone. While there may have been a symbolic element to the incorporation of older sculpture in a new church building—a widespread phenomenon elsewhere in Scotland—the most straightforward explanation is, perhaps, the need to dispose of stone cleared from the foot-print of the new building (Ewan Campbell, pers comm). For this reason it seems likely that the Latinus stone, along with all the rest of the Early Medieval sculpture, once stood on the summit of the hill, within the general area occupied by the Priory. Thomas proposed that the Latinus stone may have been cleared and built into a wall as early as the Northumbrian take-over of the site in the eighth century (1997, 40), and certainly we may imagine several episodes of site clearance and remodelling over the centuries.

Although the Latinus stone has suffered damage, there are no signs of the deliberate trimming seen on other slabs, perhaps because it was sufficiently block-shaped already. The top left corner has broken off, but the weathering of the exposed edge suggests this is an ancient loss, predating the inscription. There are scattered tool-marks across the surface indicating the stone has been struck with a pointed tool, but there is no clear patterning to these marks which are perhaps related to its apparent Medieval re-use as a building block. The incised surface of the stone is worn, particularly at the top, and this is consistent with its having stood in the open for a considerable period. A large part of the reverse of the pillar has been covered with cement into which palm-sized chunks of stone have been embedded. There is no record of when this was done but it appears to have been an attempt to strengthen the stone, perhaps when it first went on display (Stephen Gordon, Historic Scotland, pers comm).

The Stone[5]

The raw material of the Latinus stone was formed over 400 million years ago from the mud and silt which once lay at the bottom of the huge ancient ocean known as 'Iapetus'. The thrusting forces which destroyed this ocean—and created the Scottish Highlands—crushed its silty residues into sedimentary rocks known as Turbidite ('greywacke'), the dominant bedrock of south-west Scotland (see Barnes 1989). A side view of the Latinus stone reveals these silt layers—along which the rock splits naturally—now running vertically. Turbidite has a tendency to break along cleavage planes which lie at an angle to these sedimentary layers and this has been exploited in the shaping of the rectangular block, with its chamfered edges. The immense pressure involved in the formation of Turbidite created ripples through the rock. These can be seen on the Latinus stone in the undulation of the exposed carved surface.

Geologically, the Latinus stone may be characterised as 'fine-grained grey Turbidite siltstone' (see Ruckley 2004 for analysis). It is slightly different in composition—in terms of colour, grain-size and magnetic susceptibility—from the siltstones used for the bulk of the 'Whithorn School' sculptures of the tenth century, but close to the stones used for a number of other Whithorn sculptures (eg the rune-stone EC.10), including some late examples (EC.32, EC.22 =

---

[4] Pieces of sculpture from Whithorn are referred to by their Historic Scotland accession number (see Historic Scotland Guidebook, Radford and Donaldson 1953 and 1984).

[5] I am grateful to Ewan Campbell, Ray Chadburn, and Nigel Ruckley for discussing the geology with me.

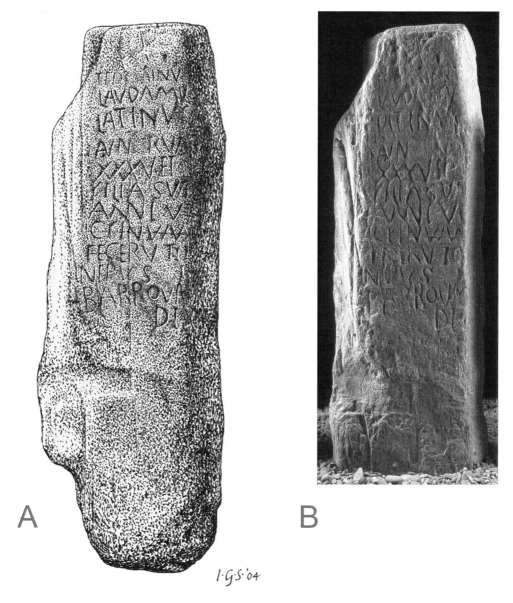

Figure 1: The Latinus Stone, Whithorn Priory Museum.
A Drawing by Ian G Scott.
B Photograph © Crown Copyright reproduced courtesy of Historic Scotland.

Boghouse 1). Unfortunately the nature of Turbidite precludes precise localisation, but comparison with other stones in the Whithorn collection suggests the Latinus stone is probably from an outcrop in the immediate vicinity.

The stone is 1.56m long. The lower third is rough and unworked, suggesting the likely depth to which it was embedded in the ground. It has two broad faces—one flat, the other convex—which have a maximum width of c0.5m. The average depth of the slab is 0.18m. The long edges of the front face are chamfered, creating a flat carving surface approximately 0.35m wide, tapering slightly at the top.

The Inscription

The inscription comprises twelve lines of Latin text occupying the full width of the front. The letters are roman capitals which vary in height from 40 to 70mm. They have been incised by

21

pecking with a round, pointed tool; the usual technique in inscriptions of this period. The inscription is complete, although worn in places, especially in the top line and at the right margin of all the longer lines. Even where there is wear, however, the reading is not in real doubt. In the following transcription, [.] indicates an illegible character, letters enclosed in square brackets are damaged but legible, letters underlined are ligatured:

TED[..]INV[M]
LAVDAMV[.]
LATINV[S]
ANN[O]RVM
XXXVET
FILIASVA
ANNI V
ICSINUM
FECERVT[N]
NEPVS
BARROVA
DI

This may be reconstructed as:

> *Te Dominum laudamus. Latinus annorum xxxv et filia sua anni v (h)ic sinum feceru<n>t nepus Barrouadi*

Leaving to one side for now the issue of *sinum* and whether or not it represents classical Latin *signum*, we may translate the above as:

> 'We praise you, the Lord ! Latinus, *nepus* ('grandson/descendant') of Barrouadus, 35 years of age, and his daughter, aged 5, here made a *si(g)num*'

Radford (1956, 174-5, fig 9) (and following him Thomas 1992a, 3) read *nipus* rather than *nepos* in the tenth line, but this is a mistake (similarly his *ficerut* for *feceru<n>t*).[6] The cross-strokes of the E are short, but they are legible, and this form of narrow E is typical of Rustic Capitals in this period. Macalister spotted that the final two letters of *fecerunt* are ligatured but the cross-stroke of the T has been placed on the first vertical of the N rather than the second, giving *fecerutn* (1936; 1945, 499-501). Radford took *anni v* as an abbreviation for *ann(orum) iv*. The lack of an abbreviation mark is not a fatal objection, but more tellingly against this reading is the clear spacing between the *I* and the *V* (cf Tedeschi (2005, 296), who also reads ANNI V). This is notable given the general lack of spacing between letters in this inscription, and is in particular contrast to the four characters in the numeral *XXXV* which are all conjoined. The formula is not unprecedented: it is found also on the roughly contemporary memorial to Rustica at Llanerfyl which expresses her age as: ANI XIII (see below for further discussion).

There is a large faint incised linear cross covering the middle third of the surface of the stone, intersecting at the *n* of *sinum*. Macalister (1936; 1945) made much of this, interpreting it as a Christian cross, the referent of *si(g)num*. As Thomas points out a cross at this early date is 'an impossible anachronism' (1992a, 3). In any case, the intersecting lines are of an entirely different nature to the lettering, being much slighter. They may be natural (there are parallel vertical lines of similar nature by the left edge). If not, they might relate to the Medieval reuse of the stone, being, perhaps, a mark of the mid-point of the stone (while still embedded in the ground), or marks made by fastenings used to topple or drag it.

---

[6] Thomas's discussion of the inscription perpetuates this reading, although he corrects it in the caption to his fig 3 (Thomas 1992a, 4).

A chi-rho ?

In correspondence and other unpublished documentation Galloway described the Latinus stone as 'bearing the *chrisma*' above the inscription (Craig 1992, 286). His sketch shows that he is referring to the chi-rho monogram (the first letters of Christ's name in Greek—XP—superimposed) in its early, 'Constantianian' form. The chi-rho predates the use of the cross as a Christian symbol and in its Constantian form dates, in Britain, to the fourth and fifth centuries, being superseded in the later fifth and sixth centuries by a form based on the cross, with vestigial 'rho' hook attached to the upright (Thomas 1981, 86-90), as seen at Kirkmadrine (Forsyth 2005, 122-6). Although Allen's photograph of the stone (Allen & Anderson 1903, fig 539) indeed appears to show something of that nature in this area, Galloway's observation was not known to subsequent writers until Derek Craig's doctoral research almost a century later. Craig was able to examine Galloway's papers, having obtained special permission since they were still at that time closed to public inspection under the official Secrets Act (!) (Craig 1992, 286). Scrutiny of the stone led Craig to endorse Galloway's identification and to identify a six-armed (ie 'Constantinian') chi-rho, approximately 10cm tall, incised above the first line of text.

Once noted, the identification seemed persuasive: there did indeed appear to be something linear and chi-rho-like in this area of the stone as it stood in the old display. I myself was happy to accept this interpretation (Forsyth 2005, 115). Not only did the apparent presence of a chi-rho provide further confirmation of the early date of the inscription, but it seemed to solve the mystery of the referent of *sinum*. Sadly, however, when it comes to inscriptions, lighting can be deceptive. The stone's temporary removal to Historic Scotland's conservation facility at South Gyle allowed more detailed inspection of the stone under controlled conditions and, after initial resistance, I was forced to concede that the 'chi-rho' is, in fact, a chimera. There is indeed a vertical incised line about 10cm long above the *–mi-* of *Dominus*, although it is not truly aligned with the text, but leans somewhat to left. The putative diagonal lines are, however, illusory.

While there are indeed some indentations in appropriate places on either side of the vertical, these do not form continuous lines. The impression of cross-strokes is partially due to local discoloration in the surface of the stone. A micro-topographical laser scan of the surface by Archaeoptics, which was able to record every lump and bump while 'filtering out' colour variation, confirmed the presence of the vertical incision but revealed no trace of any of the proposed diagonals.[7] The vertical incision appears less substantial than the lettering although this could be a function of the degree of wear increasing towards the top of the monument. The line could be a stray mark, unconnected with the fifth-century carving. As noted above, there are other percussion marks of uncertain date scattered apparently randomly across the surface. Whatever the status of the vertical, the identification of a chi-rho appears to be ruled out. By a remarkable chance, however, while conservation of the stones was underway, the RCAHMS conducted a survey of the incised carving on the walls of St Ninian's Cave, Physgyll. In the course of this John Borland discovered not only a number of previously unrecorded crosses but also a single chi-rho monogram of six-armed Constantianian shape (RCAHMS 2007). The spot on the chi-rho distribution map can thus remain over the southern tip of the Machars, albeit very slightly to the left!

Script

The palaeography of the inscription has been analysed in detail by Carlo Tedeschi and the following is based on his account (2005, 295-7). The classically inspired horizontal layout of text on the Latinus stone and the form of its script, assign it to a small group of fifth-century British inscriptions—which includes Penmachno, Mathry 1, Llangefni, and Hayle, in addition to the inscription from Llanerfyl already mentioned—which is 'still strongly dependent on the models represented by the third and fourth century British epigraphy' (Tedeschi 2001, 17).

---

[7] I am grateful to Peter Yeoman of Historic Scotland for allowing me to inspect the results of the Archaeoptics scan.

Tedeschi characterises the Latinus stone as exhibiting the following palaeographical features which are typical of Late Roman provincial epigraphy, in Britain and elsewhere: B with separated loops, R with loop separated from the stroke (in *Barrouadi*), M with outer strokes wide apart and inner strokes meeting level with the line, and L with sloping cross-stroke (both forms seen also on Mathry 1). Other distinctive features of the Latinus inscription are: F (in *filia*) with parallel strokes which slope upwards, small O (in *Barrouadi*), and the use of two forms of S—capital (as in *sua* and *nepus*) and minuscule (as in *Latinus* and *sinum*). The inscription exhibits a comparatively high number of ligatures, but this is not simply a question of lack of space—the *nn* of *anni* are ligatured even though, at five letters, this is the shortest line in the inscription (bar the final run-on)—rather it exemplifies a tendency in late Roman British epigraphy, which becomes even more pronounced in British post-Roman inscriptions, to link and combine letters (Tedeschi 2001, 17). In addition to the ligatures proper (*an*, *nn*, *nt*) there are several instances of conjoined letters, eg *xxv*, *an*, and even when separate there is often a lack of spacing between letters on the same line. Taken together these features give the script of the Latinus stone what Tedeschi calls a 'linked' appearance ('*l'aspetto "concatenate"*', Tedeschi 2005, 295).

The placing of the cross-stroke of the T in *fecerunt* on the first rather than the second down-stroke of the N may be simply a mistake, but if not, could reflect the widespread taste for reversed and inverted letters which 'becomes a sort of distinguishing mark of Early Christian epigraphy in Britain in contrast to contemporary Continental epigraphy' (Tedeschi 2001, 18). There is variation in letter-size within and between lines, and the lines themselves are neither strictly straight, parallel, nor equally spaced. Clearly they were not ruled prior to carving, although attention has been given to align the left margin. In comparison with later inscriptions (of the sixth and seventh centuries), however, the layout of the lettering is regular, even, and dense and indicates some familiarity with late Roman traditions of textual layout.

Reading

Invocation

The text begins with a two-line invocation: *Te dominum | laudamus* 'We praise you, the Lord!'. This is a unique formula, unparalled in Early Medieval epigraphy. It is significant that *dominum* is written out in full. In the Christian Latin tradition it was normal practice in writing to abbreviate the *nomina sacra*, the group of half a dozen terms central to worship which comprised various names of the godhead. The practice involved taking the first and final letters of the sacred name, the latter varying according to case: *d̄s* (*deus*), *d̄m̄* (*deum*), etc. It began in the fourth century with *deus*, *iesus*, *christus* and *spiritus*, to which was added, 'almost simultaneously' abbreviations for *dominus* (Bischoff 1990, 152). Early epigraphic examples of this *nomen sacrum* are found in Kerry, on probably seventh-century inscribed cross-slabs from the monastic sites of Reask (*d̄n̄s*, *d̄n̄e* and *d̄n̄o*) and Kilmalkedar (*d̄n̄e* and *d̄n̄i*) (Okasha and Forsyth 2001, 175-82, 165-71). The lack of abbreviation on the Latinus stone is consistent with the fifth-century date proposed below, and indeed may point to a date earlier rather than later in that century. Moreover, it may suggest that the Christian community at Whithorn was not familiar with the latest ecclesiastical scribal practice and was not using recently copied bibles. The composer of the Reask and Kilmalkedar inscriptions expected his predominantly monastic audience to recognise and decode the abbreviations. No such assumption was made of the audience of the Latinus stone, perhaps simply because it was a predominantly secular one, literate but not learned.

Previous writers have taken the phrase *Te dominum laudamus* to be a quotation from a liturgical text of some sort but it has thus far proved impossible to identify (Thomas 1992a, 6; Tedeschi 2005, 295). Radford took the phrase as an allusion to Psalm 145 v.2: *Laudabo Dominum in vita mea* (1956, 173), or alternatively to *Laudate dominum*, the opening words of Psalm 146: 'Praise ye the Lord, Praise the Lord, O my soul, While I live will I praise the Lord', which formed part of the Roman office for the Dead (Radford and Donaldson 1984, 27). A much closer verbal parallel, however, is the opening line of the Ambrosian hymn:[8]

> Te deum laudamus; te dominum confitemur.
> Te aeternum patrem omnis terra veneratur….

> 'We praise thee, O God ; we acknowledge thee to be the Lord
> All the earth doth worship thee, the Father everlasting….

This, the 'Te Deum', was one of the best-known Latin hymns of praise. In later legend its composition was attributed to Ambrose and Augustine in 387, it was, however, probably written by the fourth-century Bishop Nicetas of Remesiana (c*335–414*). It is sung to this day as part of the liturgy for Sundays and on other occasions in thanksgiving to God for a special blessing (eg consecration of a bishop, the canonization of a saint, the profession of a religious) (Henry 1912). The earliest extant text of the 'Te deum' appears in the Antiphonary of Bangor, a late seventh-century liturgical commonplace book written at Bangor, Co. Down (Kenney 1929, 707-12) where it is known as *Ymnum in die dominica* 'The Sunday hymn' (Curran 1984). As it stands, the invocation on the Latinus stone is, obviously, not a quotation of the 'Te deum' (although in conflating the two opening phrases it could nonetheless be an allusion to the hymn). Alternatively, it is possible there has been some confusion. If the composer of the inscription was familiar with the 'Te deum' from a written text (rather than having learnt it orally), he would have seen the opening line written thus: *Te dm̄ laudamus*, using the standard abbreviation of the *nomen sacrum*. Confusion of *dm̄* and *dn̄m* is common enough in later manuscripts and it would be an easy error to expand *dm̄* as *dominum*.[9] If this were the case, it would make the Latinus stone the earliest attestation of the text by two centuries, or more.[10] Of course, the inscription may quote a lost text, or may not be a quotation at all. On balance, this is perhaps the most likely explanation. The formula of address, using not the vocative but 'Te + accusative', is well established and the sentiment an appropriate one. In all probability then, the entire text of the inscription was composed for the occasion at Whithorn. The Te Deum parallel indicates that such a composition was in keeping with contemporary liturgical taste.

Latinus

Following the invocation, the rest of the text begins with the name of the principal commemorand: Latinus. The name occupies the whole of that line and is written in letters slightly larger than those of the preceding and succeeding lines. This combines to give it a visual prominence often accorded the name of the principal in Early medieval inscriptions.[11] The name is—emphatically!—a Latin one, well-attested in Roman Britain[12] and Roman and post-Roman Gaul.[13] It is known elsewhere in post-Roman Britain from a bilingual Latin/ogham stone from North Cornwall, at Worthyvale, near Tintagel. The female version *Latina* survived into medieval Welsh as *Lledin* (Sims-Williams 2003, 185).

While it may appear to us to be the most 'Latin' of Latin names, it is difficult to gauge what connotations it had for contemporaries. Henry Gough-Cooper suggests to me its popularity among Celtic-Speakers may in part derive from its superficial similarity to the native word 'hero' (Gaulish *latis,* Old Irish *láth*) (pers comm). As Sims-Williams notes, this is well-attested as a personal name, both as a simplex, *Lat(t)ius*, and in compounds, such as *Andolatius* and

---

[8] I owe this insight to my colleague, Gilbert Márkus.

[9] I owe this ingenious suggestion to Prof Tom O'Loughlin.

[10] And, in European terms, strikingly close to the place of next attestation, Bangor, Co. Down.

[11] For this practice on a different stone see Higgitt 2001.

[12] On a grave in Bath of a soldier from Nyon (RIB i 158), and on a building stone from Hadrian's Wall (RIB i 1409), and on pieces of pottery, including Samian ware from Corbridge (RIB vii 2501.565), Winchester (RIB viii 2503.303) and elsewhere (RIB viii 2505.12), and, closest to home, on an oculist's stamp from Tranent, Inveresk (RIB iv 2446.12), see also RIB v 2491.101.

[13] For instance, as Henry Gough-Cooper has pointed out to me (pers com), as the name of one archbishop of Tours (Duchesne II.308).

Segolatius (2003, 185 n.1122). Nevertheless it is clear that Latin names were adopted with enthusiasm by Romano-Britons and that many were incorporated into the stock of British names which continued in use among the Britons throughout the Middle Ages (and indeed till the present). The most famous examples of this process are, perhaps, Arthur (< *Artorius*), Patrick (< *Patricius*), and Emrys (< *Ambrosius*). The considerable popularity of such 'continuing-Roman' names is reflected in the frequency with which they appear on 'Group 1' inscriptions in western Britain. Nearly a quarter (23%) of the names on these stones are of Latin origin (Sims-Williams 2002, 15-22). Examples from the fifth-century stones discussed above include Rustica and her father *Paterninus*, *Porius*, and *Saturninus*. Although they became linguistically 'naturalised' into British/Welsh, these names must have retained a specific connotation because there is a marked drop in their frequency on inscriptions of the seventh century onwards (down to about 6%), when they appear to have been rejected *as a class* in favour of the old traditional Celtic names, such as *Catamanus* (Cadfan). We would not expect this if they had been adopted without distinction into the pool of names. Thus the adoption of Latin names reflects a conscious cultural alignment which eventually lost its currency or appeal.

That names of Roman origin were similarly popular not only within the confines of the former province but also beyond the old Imperial *limes* is hinted at in later Welsh texts which purport to relate to the 'Old North' in this period. The genealogies assign several names of Latin origin to Northern dynasts of these generations: Patern son of Tacit < *Paternus*, *Tacitus*; Cinhil son of Cluim < *Quintilius*, *Clemens*; Aircol son of Triphun < *Agricola*, *Tribunus* (Bartrum (ed) 1966, 9-11). The Gododdin poems contain a reference to *gorsedd Senyllt* 'the mound/court of Senyllt' (A.47 = Williams 1938 CA 1). The figure of Senyllt (< *Senilius*) also appears in the Welsh Triads (Bromwich (ed) 1961, 5). The value of such late literary evidence for sub-Roman northern Britain is much debated but unambiguous contemporary evidence of the adoption of Roman names is seen in southern Scotland on several inscriptions: the fifth-century inscription at Kirkliston (The Cat Stane), commemorates the child of *Victricius*, and, from the sixth century, the inscription from Brox, Liddesdale, commemorates *Carantius* son of *Cupitianus*, and that at Kirkmadrine, Galloway, *Viventius* and *Florentius*. The Britons of the North are thus seen, in this respect at least, to be utterly in keeping with their British cousins further south.

Nepus Barrouadi

After the head of an inscription, the next most visually prominent position is its foot, and on our stone this is occupied by the other personal name, that of Latinus's ancestor Barrouados. Again the letters are slightly larger than those of the main body of the text, even though this has entailed a run-on of the two final letters. This is the only run-on in the whole inscription: elsewhere line-ends coincide with word-ends. Given that the nine letter *Barrouadi* was going to require more than one line, it would have been possible to start it immediately after the –*s* of *nepus*, and fill out the remaining space on that line before concluding the name on a final line, ending at or near the right margin. Instead a gap was left and the new name begun on a line of its own, thus making it stand out (and easy to point out to the illiterate or semi-literate). There seem no grounds for accepting Radford's assertion that the final lines '*nepus Barrouadi*' are secondary. There is no obvious distinction in carving technique or letter forms and the somewhat 'detached' syntax may, as suggested above, have been determined by a desire to place 'Barrouados' in text-final position.

The name *Barrouados* is a Celtic one (it could be either British or Gaelic). Although not otherwise attested, it is formed from the well known personal-name element **barro*- 'point', 'head', which was particularly favoured by Irish speakers but is also attested among the British. Sims-Williams gives a number of epigraphic examples (2003, 77 n.360), including compounds with *cuno*- 'hound': British BARCUNI (364/144), and its inverse, the possibly Irish CONBARRUS (324/34) (also attested in the Roman period by CUNOBARRUS RIB ii 2416.4); and, compounded with *uendo*- 'fair, white': BARRIUENDI (368/150) which gives Irish *Bairrfhind*, and Welsh *Berwyn/Barwyn*, and its inverse UENDUBARI which gives Irish *Finnbarr*. (For **Barro*- in ogham inscriptions see Ziegler 1994, 99-100.)

The identity of the second element of *Barro-uados* is not certain. In an unpublished note quoted by Sims-Williams (2003, 120 n.664), Kenneth Jackson (1953) suggested 'mole' (**uad-*, Welsh *gwadd*) which appears in the name GUADAN on a much later Welsh inscription (979/46). If the name is British, 'mole-head', then the *-o-* is the linguistically 'correct' composition vowel. If it were Gaelic we might expect *Barriuadi*, but as Sims-Williams states, in such a case the *-o-* could be due to the labial environment (2003, 120), and so the name is not conclusively diagnostic one way or the other. Sims-Williams assigns it to his category 'possibly Irish' (2003, 422). Thomas proposed a 'possibly Primitive Irish **Barro-wedas*' (1992b, 6), but, as Sims-Williams notes, 'that reconstruction has the wrong vowel' (Sims-Williams 2003, 120). The form *Barrouados* is an early one, exhibiting neither the sound change apocope (loss of final syllables) nor that of syncope (loss of medial syllables) (Sims-Williams 2003, 320), and is thus consistent with the fifth-century date indicated by palaeography.

Contrary to Radford's view (Radford and Donaldson 1953, 36) *'nepus Barrouadi'* refers not to a descendant of Latinus (who erected the monument) but to his ancestor. Latin *nepos* means 'grandson', but also, more broadly 'descendant.' The spelling *nepus* for Classical Latin *nepos* reflects the well-attested Late Latin confusion of *u* for *o*, seen on other sub-Roman western British inscriptions (T Charles-Edwards 1995, 718; Sims-Williams 2003, 42; Jackson 1953, 191). In Irish literary sources of the early Middle Ages *nepos* is used interchangeably with Irish *moccu* to signify membership of a kingroup or *gens* (T Charles-Edwards 1993, 156-7). Latin *nepos* is thus the exact equivalent of Irish *aue* (genitive *aui*) 'grandson, descendant', which was used on ogham inscriptions in addition to or instead of the more normal patronymic, and in its later form, *ua* (pl. *uí*), was used as a common designation of kindred, eg *Uí Neill* (O'Neil) = Latin *nepotis Nellis*. Thus *Latinus nepus Barrouadi* could mean 'L. grandson of B.', or 'L. of the kindred of B.' (the equivalent of ogham *Latini aui Barrouadi*, or of a seventh – eighth-century manuscript *Latinus moccu Barrouadi*). It is tempting to see this as a distinctively Irish way of identifying people, but the only other example of the epigraphic use of *nepos* in Britain (as a word rather than a *cognomen*)[14] is on the monument of a man identified as a Caledonian (Lossio Ueda's early-third-century dedicatory plaque, from Colchester, RIB 191). Thus, despite the many Roman features of his monument, Latinus is identified in traditional native fashion.

et filia sua

Memorials to women of any sort represent only a tiny proportion of the Group I inscriptions of Western Britain (there are none among the early Irish ogham pillars), and commemorations of females identified as daughters, rather than wives, are rarer still. The monument to the girl Rustica at Llanerfyl has been mentioned already, and to it may be added those of the daughters Velvoria at Llandysul, Cardiganshire, and Avitoria at Eglwys Gymyn, Carmarthenshire (the gender of Vetta commemorated on the Catstane, although previously identified as feminine, is, in fact, not certain: Sims-Williams 2003, 135). What is unique about the Latinus stone, however, is that it is a memorial to a daughter *and* her father. Single memorials to more than one person are very rare within the post-Roman corpus. Apart from the late Group 1 memorial to a pair of brothers from Yarrowkirk, Selkirkshire, most of the handful of exceptions are early joint memorials to married couples. There is one other example of the pairing of a parent and child: the lost ogham/latin bi-lingual monument to Cantianus and his father, the Irish-named, Maccutrenos, from Llywel (Crai) in Brecknockshire. In this example, however, it is the father who is identified with reference to the son (*'et pater illius'*) rather than, as here, the child identified with reference to her father. Indeed, she is identified only by reference to her father; it is a striking feature of the Whithorn inscription that the name of the daughter is not given. Why mention her but not name her?

---

[14] There is a single sub-Roman instance of *pronepos*, 'great-grandson', spelled *pronepus*, on the later sixth-century *Boduoc* stone from Margam Mountain, Glamorganshire, which identifies the British-named Boduoc as the son of 'Catotigirni' and *pronepos* of 'Eternali Uedomaui'.

The monuments to Rustica and Latinus's daughter are certainly (and those to Avitoria and Velvoria possibly) memorials to children, and belong to the very tail end of the Roman monumental tradition in which the commemoration of children, especially young children, was not uncommon (see index to RIB I). From c500 there is a shift in emphasis among the western British stones towards the commemoration of adult males almost exclusively. After this date no children, and few, if any, women are commemorated. This reflects a change in the role of inscribed monuments, away from the personal and sentimental towards the dynastic and proprietorial (Handley 1998; Forsyth 2005).

At thirteen years we may assume that Rustica would have been unmarried, like the five-year old daughter of Latinus. Although the ages of Avitoria and Velvoria are not stated, it is perhaps likely that they too, were unmarried, as only in special cirumstances would a married woman be formally identified by reference to her father rather than her husband. There is a unique epigraphic example of the commemoration of married women as daughters: a lost stone from Llanymawdwy (Caer Gai), Merioneth, which is exceptional in several respects. It is a joint memorial to a pair of sisters who are identified both with reference to their own husbands (who are named) and their common father Salvianus. These women are primarily identified as daughters, only secondarily as wives, and it is possible the monument is an assertion of land-rights following an atypical inheritance via the female line in the absence of any sons of Salvianus.

Annorum, anni(s)

The expression of age, like the commemoration of children, is a feature of Roman memorial epigraphy which is represented only on the earliest of the British Christian memorials. The age of the deceased is stated on three such monuments: Whithorn, Llanerfyl, and Hayle. The latter uses the standard Roman formula: 'VIXIT ANNOS' seen, for instance, on late Roman inscriptions from Brougham (RIB 787), Maryport (RIB 862-3) and Old Carlisle (RIB 908). The other two diverge from this pattern. The Llanerfyl text gives Rustica's age using the ablative case: *ani xiii* (for *annis xiii*). The spelling *an(n)i* for *annis* reflects the loss of final *–s* seen in some areas of Romance, including British Latin (as attested by a number of examples of *–i* for *–is* on sub-Roman Western British inscriptions, eg 413/272, 416/279, 402/184, 418/283; see T Charles-Edwards 1995, 716). The same formula is found at Whithorn for the age of Latinus's daughter, given as *anni v*. The age of Latinus himself is given in a different way, using the genitive: *annorum xxxv*. Both forms are grammatically correct and—unless some semantic distinction, now opaque, is intended—the variation appears to be merely stylistic.

(H)ic

The variant spelling *ic* for *hic* is seen on a dozen stones from Wales and Cornwall. In the phrase *ic iacit* it appears on 324/34, 325/33, 327/43, 344/73, 353/127, 395/102, 401/183, 470/Ok.78 (Worthyvale) and 483/Ok.51. On its own *ic* appears on 462/Ok.14, 1057/Ok.54, and -/Ok.4.[15]

Si(g)num

The one remaining uncertainty concerning the reading is the meaning of *sinum*. The Latin word *sĭnus, -us* means a 'bent or curved surface', and hence has a range of meanings such as 'bay of the sea', 'valley/hollow in the land'. Soutar even notes its use by the Christian author Cassiodorus to refer to a shelf (in a library) (1949, s.v.). In Classical Latin it was used to refer to the hanging fold in the upper part of the toga, and, by extension 'bosom', and hence, more metaphorically, 'love', 'protection'. Thomas took the *sinum* of the Latinus inscription as this word. Extending its meaning yet further he interpreted *sinum* here as meaning 'shelter in the bosom of the Lord' and 'refuge from the non-Christian world outside', in otherwords, as 'yet another synonym for church' (1992a, 6). Certainly, expressions such as *sinus (matris) Ecclesiae*

---

[15] See the reading of Tedeschi 2005, 253.

are amply attested, but these refer to the 'bosom of the Church' in a metaphorical sense, not in the concrete sense of a church building. Thomas himself concedes that *sinus* is not attested among the several Early Christian words for a church building. A metaphorical usage would be quite unexpected among the vocabulary of early British inscriptions which is otherwise, limited and concrete: *memoria, locus, in tumulo, in congeries lapidum*.

It seems less problematic to follow all other writers in taking *sinum* as a variant of *signum* 'sign'.[16] Thomas objects that *sinum* is not found for *signum*, yet he refers to an early Christian inscription from Rome mentioned by Radford (1956, 174) which has exactly that: *sinnum posuit* 'placed this sign (ie memorial stone)' (Diehl 1927, 248 no 3630; see also no.3518: *zinnum loci*). The identification of the *signum* as the putative chi-rho must now be rejected (as discussed above). MacQueen (1990) took it more metaphorically, as a 'sign', possibly a 'miracle' and indeed the word is attested with this meaning in Gregory of Tours' History of the Franks (Souter 1949 s.v.; Niermeyer 1976 s.v.). I would, however, propose a more straightforward interpretation, namely that *sinum* (for *signum*) means here 'stone monument', as it does in the aforementioned example from Rome. *Signum* is found with this meaning in Roman Britain, referring, for instance, to a statue in Cirencester, Gloucestershire (RIB 103) and a statue-base from Birrens, Dumfriesshire (RIB 2103) where the phrase is: *sign(um) posuerunt* 'set up this statue'. That *signum* continued to be understood in this sense is indicated by an eighth- or ninth-century stone cross-shaft from Yarm, North Riding of Yorkshire (now in Durham Cathedral Library) which bears an inscription in Anglo-Saxon stating that the principal **signum** *aefter his breodera ssetae*, 'set up this monument in memory of his brother' (Okasha 1971, 130, no.145).[17] This example is notable in employing a Latin loanword in preference to the more usual, vernacular *beacon*. Radford cites Ducange's Glossary of Medieval and Late Latin (s.v. *Signum* (3)) for the Medieval use of the word to mean, specifically, 'boundary stone' (1956, 174). It appears with this meaning in the mid-seventh-century Lex Visigothorum (Book 10.3; see Niermeyer 1976, 971). There appears, therefore to be ample grounds for translating Latinus' *sinum* (for *signum*) as 'monument'.

Fecerunt

Thomas correctly pointed out that the Latinus stone does not explicitly identify itself as a tomb or grave-marker, nor refer to the deaths of the people involved (1992a, 6). In his opinion it was not, therefore, primarily funerary, but rather recorded a gift of land to the church. He envisioned it standing by the entrance to a church where, 'in its Christian commemoration of the donors of the plot or the recent benefactors, it would be a rustic counterpart of a *titulus* slab on some grander edifice in metropolitan Italy or Gaul' (1992a, 6). His scenario is not entirely without parallels: we do have two, albeit later, inscriptions commemorating the donation of plots of land, apparently for cemeteries: these are the seventh- and early eighth-century inscribed cross-slabs from Llanllyr, Cardiganshire (993/124) (Handley 2001b) and Kilnasaggart, Armagh (CIIC 946). Both texts, however, explicitly mention the act of giving/bequeathing with the appropriate verb (respectively, Latin *dedit*, and Old Irish *tanimmairni*). More importantly, these monuments belong to a quite different (learned, ecclesiastical) tradition and to a later period when the church and its scriptoria were well-established.

The sixth-century majority of the 'Group 1' inscriptions are quite rigidly and narrowly formulaic. In contrast, the earliest (ie fifth-century) stratum displays considerable diversity, as if the tradition were still at an experimental phase. Although some words and phrases recur, each of the extant early texts is unique in composition. A small number of possibly early examples consist of a name only (or name with filiation), but of the majority which go beyond this, all contain an explicitly funerary or sepulchral word or phrase drawn from the common pool of late Antique Christian epigraphy: most commonly *hic (in tumulo) iacit*, but also others, for instance *memoria*. The extremely worn inscription from Hayle (Carnsew) extravagantly uses three

---

[16] There is also a different word *sīnum* (n), 'large earthenware pot', but this is unlikely to be relevant here.
[17] I'm grateful to Dr. David Parsons, Univ. of Nottingham, for drawing my attention to this inscription.

separate such phrases, when any one might have sufficed: *hic pacem requievit, hic tumulo iacit, visxit annos xxx[iii]*. The sole exception to this funerary phraseology is the Latinus stone, with its statement that Latinus and his daughter 'here made a monument'. Certainly this is unprecedented, but the giving of ages strongly points to a funerary context (Tedeschi 2005, 495), as Thomas himself concedes (1992a, 6). Explicitly funerary formulae were not essential to inscribed memorials: although a large number of sixth- and seventh-century Western British inscriptions have (*hic*) *iacit*, the majority are name-only; and in Ireland the overwhelming majority of ogham inscriptions have names (and kinship terms) only.[18] The funerary function of these monuments is borne out by such archaeological evidence as we have. In the small number of cases where the original location of sub-Roman British inscriptions is believed to be known they appear to have stood beside burials, either single graves in landscape contexts (eg Clocaenog, Hayle, Trawsfynnyd) or in cemeteries (eg the Cat Stane, and perhaps Mathry) (see further below). The Latinus stone itself comes from what became an important cemetery. The weight of comparison is therefore strongly against it being anything other than a funerary monument.

Dating

Evidence for dating is provided by three aspects of the Latinus stone: the form of script, the spelling of the names, and the general form of monument. The palaeography of the inscription, as discussed above, indicates a date in the fifth century. The form of the script used belongs to Tedeschi's 'First Phase' which consists of inscriptions 'which present more or less the same letter-forms—even if exaggerated—as British Late Antique epigraphy' (2001, 24). This phase is unlikely to be any *earlier* than the fifth century because these inscriptions 'though showing clear similarities with the epigraphy of the fourth century, represent a further step in the evolution of the writing' (*ibid*). The Latinus stone is unlikely to be any *later* than the fifth century as it lacks any of the features which characterise Tedeschi's 'Second Phase' which he dates to the first half of the sixth century (namely, R with increasingly horizontal slanting stroke, N with elongated first stroke, horizontal I, etc). The dating provided by palaeography is therefore: 'within the fifth century'.

The form of the only non-Latin part of the inscription, the Celtic personal-name Barrouados, reflects an early stage of the language, before the loss of final syllables, which is consistent with this early date, but cannot refine it further.

As discussed above, various aspects of the monument and its text draw on the Late Roman epigraphic tradition. The scale of the lettering (relative to the monument) and its horizontal layout (a mode largely abandoned in the sixth and early seventh centuries in favour of verticality) recall Roman milestones. The stating of the ages of the deceased and the commemoration of children (and females) are both features well-attested in the Roman tradition but which quickly die out in the post-Roman period. In general terms, the Latinus stone reflects an epigraphic tradition which has moved on since the Late Roman period, but not far.

Some authorities have attempted to narrow the dating. Radford, for instance, cites R G Collingwood's opinion that it was erected not later than the first half of the fifth century, though qualifies this by saying that he himself 'could not exclude the second half of the century' (Collingwood & Wright 1965, 175).[19] Unfortunately such attempts at refinement are probably futile. The oft-repeated date 'c450' is just a guess, the reality could be close to 400 or close to 500. We simply do not know how quickly script developed in this period and should resist the urge to plump for one bit of the fifth century over another. Yet, whatever the absolute date, in

---

[18] The exception being late examples with *anm* and the small number with *koi*, the meaning of which is disputed, see Swift 1997.

[19] Jackson's dating 'beginning of the sixth century' on the grounds of the spelling *nepus* for *nepos* does not seem justified (1953, 191).

relative terms the above features combine to indicate that the Latinus stone is likely to be amongst the earliest of the whole corpus of post-Roman British inscriptions.

Discussion

The sub-group of early inscribed stones to which Latinus belongs are datable to the fifth century by the form of their scripts, but they are also united by certain shared features which distinguish them from their successors in the sixth century and later. Their texts are generally longer, some of them significantly longer than the later ones, and contain various additional words and phrases beyond the short and simple statements of name and filiation found later. The results are diverse, each text is unique. The fifth century-western British inscriptions reflect an initial, experimental phase, before the tradition settled on the more narrowly formulaic format of the sixth and seventh centuries. It is as if at this stage the elite were still casting around for available materials from which to construct a new monumental tradition. A major resource was the local Late Roman tradition of monumental epigraphy, which supplied, not only the basic idea of lapidary monuments, but also details of layout and phrasing. The fifth-century inscriptions, however, are not merely imitations of old Roman forms. Circumstances had changed and new monumental forms were evolving to meet them. The physicality of these monuments, and their landscape setting, represents a departure from Roman practice and draws instead on a much more ancient native monumental tradition, that of the prehistoric standing stone. Contemporary Christian inscriptions on the Continent, which represent an unbroken continuation of Roman epigraphy, are typically plaques of modest size, commissioned by a comparatively broad social spectrum and would have been encountered in large numbers in urban cemeteries. The western British inscriptions, in contrast, were large and exceptional pillars, standing alone in the landscape or singly in rural cemeteries. A well-documented example is the Cat Stane from Kirkliston, Midlothian. Its text was carved on what may be a reused Bronze Age menhir, which formed a focus for burials in an early inhumation cemetery (Rutherford and Ritchie 1974; Cowie 1978). The next stage in the familiar development from single 'special' grave to cemetery to church, is reflected in Welsh examples from chapels such as Llantrisaint (Capel Bronwen) and parish churches, such as Penmachno (*Carausius*), Llanerfyl (*Rustica*), Llandsadwrn (*Saturninus* and his wife), and Llangefni (*Culidorix* and his wife). It would be wrong to assume that there was necessarily a church at these sites at the time the stones were erected. Certainly there are a number of Welsh examples which are far from any early church. Perhaps the most famous example is the monument to *Porius* at Trawsfynydd, Merionethshire, the location of which is described as follows:

> The place where Porius was laid to rest is on the edge of a huge expanse of bleak moorland being at a height of just over 1,000 feet above sea level and appears to the eye as if it were at the back of beyond. It is, however, exactly the point of one of the major ancient crossroads in north Wales where an early trade route running east to west from the head-waters of the river Severn to the coast, and a sea-passage to Ireland, was crossed by the main north to south Roman road, the *Sarn Helen*. These two lines of communication were in regular use until the early years of the nineteenth century (Gresham 1985, 389).

This relationship to important routeways (often old Roman roads) appears to be a defining characteristic of the location of many of these earliest monuments. A further Welsh example is the 1.98m tall monument to *Voteporix* at Castell Dwyran, found in a secondary location, 200m south of the Roman road running west to Carmarthen. In this light, the pertinent fact explaining the location of Rustica's memorial at Llanerfyl may be, not its later status as the site of the parish church, but its position on the old Roman road, east-west across the mountains of central Wales. A Scottish example of roadside location is the Cat Stane which was situated beside an old road at a river crossing (Forsyth 2005, 118). These were monuments to be seen as one moved around the landscape, at nodal points in the system of communications.

The Latinus stone appears to fit this pattern of roadside burial. There is little archaeological evidence of activity at Whithorn before AD 500 (other than the stone itself), all of the small quantity of Roman material from the site came from later layers (Hill 1997, 74, 292-3). The earliest evidence is a broad roadway crossing the site from the east end of the hill and running roughly south-west to north-east. Dating it 'earlier than the late fifth century', the excavator suggested it might have been heading to a coastal landing-point, either at Isle of Whithorn or Physgill (*ibid*, 26). A large prostrate stone slab was discovered a little to the north which, if not natural, was proposed as a possibly slighted prehistoric monument (*ibid*, 27, 74-76). If the Latinus stone originally stood near the top of the hill it would appear to have stood beside this road. From the sixth century this area was occupied by an inhumation cemetery (*ibid*, 552-6).

What remains to be explained is why this particular point in the road was chosen. One possibility is that it occupied a boundary location. The Cat Stane stands at the boundary of the Medieval parish of Kirkliston, which itself is thought to reflect a pre-existing unit of secular administration centred on the power centre commemorated in the place-name which includes the British element *lis*, cf Welsh *llys* 'court, hall' (Forsyth 2005, 118). This model is particularly attractive in the light of the meaning 'boundary-marker' for *signum* noted above. An alternative explanation is proximity to a secular power centre. The monument to the Irish-named *Cunaide* formerly stood on a mound over an oriented cist grave, just outside and below the small coastal fort of Carnsew at Hayle in north Cornwall (Thomas 1994, 190-94). Carnsew, with its commanding view of the Hayle estuary, is a short distance, c1.6km, from the important early church site of Phillack (*ibid*, 198-9). That the environs of the fort were favoured over the church underlines the close connection this group of monuments has with secular power.

An emphasis on descent (and comparative lack of female commemorations) is the norm in the later ('proprietorial') inscriptions, yet over half the fifth-century examples have no mention of filiation or ancestry. The Latinus stone is therefore somewhat unusual among the fifth-century inscriptions in providing information about the deceased's forebears. Thomas states that we are told that Latinus was *nepos Barrouadi* 'as we might learn of so-and-so that he was a great-great-grandson of Queen Victoria' (1992a, 6). In fact, far from being simply additional biographical colour, the statement of ancestry may be, in some sense, the inscription's raison d'etre for it constitutes an assertion of rights by the members of a kin-group, the *nepotes Barrouadi*. We must remember that it was not Latinus who put up the monument, but his surviving relatives, his son(s), perhaps, or his brothers and cousins—the grandsons of Barrouados—, all of whom would be members of the same three-generational kin-group which was the basic legal unit for inheritance purposes under Welsh and Irish law (T Charles-Edwards 1995; Kelly 1988). It is worth noting that the inscription does not record the name of Latinus's father, only that of his grandfather (or more distant ancestor) Barrouados. This raises the suspicion that it was his co-lateral rather than direct descendants who put up the monument. If this were the case, then it might help explain the puzzling mention of his unnamed daughter. If the girl had been included because of the Roman vogue for the 'sentimental' commemoration of young children, then surely her relatives would have named her. That she was not named suggests her importance was less in her own right as an individual than as a point in the family tree (as it were). In other words, to record her death alongside that of her father put on record that Latinus's direct line had been extinguished. There could be no future claimants through the female line, such as there appear to have been by the grandsons of Salvianus. Instead the way was clear for the sons of his cousins.

Each inscribed monument of Group 1 constitutes a physical assertion, in perpetuity, of the kin-group's association with the place, and from this, its rights to land (Handley 1998). This function cannot be separated from the burial function of such monuments. Family burial grounds in this period before the church had asserted a monopoly over Christian burial were often situated on boundaries. The buried ancestors witnessed and protected the boundary (T Charles-Edwards 1976). By recording the ancestral names in writing, relatives might hope to prevent future rival claims: there are numerous examples from the Early Irish law tracts of ogham-inscribed pillars being invoked as witnesses in disputes over land-ownership (McManus

1991 163-5). In erecting the monument to Latinus, the grandsons of Barrouados have attempted to draw on the lingering authority implied by a formal inscription in the Roman manner.

Such claims to Romanitas embodied by the sub-Roman inscriptions of western Britain are not merely aspirational. Analysis of the spelling irregularities on the Welsh monuments has showed that for the people who erected them Latin was a spoken language alongside the lower status British (T Charles-Edwards 1995, 717) and on this evidence we must accept that the elite of west Wales were bi-lingual in the fifth and sixth centuries. Many would bridle at the notion that Latin was the everyday language of the elite of Wigtownshire in this period, yet the text of the Latinus stone points in that direction. The form of words used in the inscription is not simply a standard template into which appropriate personal names could be dropped. It is an original composition. The attempt at elegance embodied by the use of two different ways of stating a person's age suggests that knowledge of Latin at Whithorn went beyond the most basic level. More tellingly, in its spelling, the text exhibits one of the features identified by Thomas Charles-Edwards as reflecting spoken Latin in Wales: loss of final –s (*anni* for *annis*). If accepted as representing *signum*, the spelling *sinum* may be additional evidence of pronunciation-spelling. It appears therefore that this was Latin not learned from a grammar book, as it would be in later centuries, but still a spoken language, at least among the elite. The choice of an *inscribed* monument over other forms of commemoration shows there was a local audience for whom such a thing would be meaningful.

That other aspects of Latinity may have been embedded in the elite culture of sub-Roman Galloway is suggested by the lettering of the inscription which reflects a familiarity with contemporary norms of Latin writing beyond a basic knowledge of capital script.

The use of minuscule *s* indicates knowledge of Roman cursive script and suggests the use of Latin writing for other purposes less formal than monumental epigraphy. The spacing of the letters in the Latinus inscription demonstrates an awareness of formal layout traditions. This contrasts with many of the Welsh monuments in which each letter appears to have been written, with some difficulty and in isolation, without attention to its relationship with its neighbours (D G Charles-Edwards 2006, 193). In this respect the Latinus stone is one of the best executed Group 1 inscriptions we have.

It is now understood that the minuscule letter-forms on the early post-Roman inscriptions of Britian are not a borrowing from contemporary Continental book-hands but an indigenous inheritance from cursive scripts of the Roman period (Edwards 2007, 45; see Tedeschi 2001 and D G Charles-Edwards 2006, 2007). Gifford Charles-Edwards has made clear that what was transmitted was the 'common writing' of stylus-writers on wax tablets, and of artificers, especially metalworkers, who were used to punching letters on hard surfaces. It is the kind of literacy that would have been familiar in a Roman military context, whether from the writing of military diplomata, or the labelling of personal kit (2006, 32, 42). Despite its Christian context, the Latinus stone reflects this non-ecclesiastical, non-manuscript post-Roman tradition of 'common writing'.

It has been argued above that in diverse respects the Latinus stone constitutes evidence of a considerable degree of 'Romanitas' among the population of Whithorn in the fifth century. The question is: is this vestigial (ie a survival of the local culture in the Roman period—which begs the question of the degree of Romanitas in the South-west in third and fourth centuries) or is it something first sought and acquired only in the fifth century (which begs the question of the accessibility of 'Roman' culture in the period after the collapse of Imperial rule)? The obvious source of Roman culture is the militarised zone around Hadrian's Wall (see McCarthy, this volume). Although the end of the wall is some distance from Whithorn overland, maritime contact with the westernmost part of this zone would have been relatively easy: the Roman naval installation at Maryport on the Cumbrian coast is, after all, visible from the Isle of Whithorn. The nature of the population in fourth century Maryport is reflected in a small clutch of late Roman inscriptions (RIB 856, 862-3). Two are written somewhat informally across plain slabs and commemorate people with Celtic names, one of them a woman, using the *vixit annos* formula. There is a high likelihood that these people were Christian. The third, a more formal stone, now lost, featured a Constantinian chi-rho. These three may be compared with an inscription from Old Carlisle which also commemorates a woman with a Celtic name, with the *vixit annos* formula (RIB 908). Continuity from the Roman period is also attested from the Wall itself at the fort of Chesterholm (Uindolanda) where a Christian church appears to have been built on top of Roman military buildings. The fifth-century inscription from this site commemorates a man with a traditionally heroic Celtic name, *Brigomaglos*, using a Christian funerary formula. These northern inscriptions represent an epigraphic bridge between the Roman and immediately post-Roman world.

It may at first seem puzzling that the earliest and most 'Roman' of the post-Roman British inscriptions should appear in places like west Cornwall, Snowdonia, and Galloway, places on the extreme periphery of the province of Britannia, with little or no trace of Roman material culture. Yet perhaps it was in such places that Romanitas could not be taken for granted, as it might further east, but had to be actively asserted. This was a period in which new identities were being forged. The old order had collapsed and the political structures of the Empire were being replaced by new, more local structures of power. New elites were competing to establish alternative sources of authority. One such source was the lingering prestige of the Empire, its language, and culture, but there were others, including militarism and heroic culture. The terms 'Roman' and 'Romanitas' are perhaps, therefore, a bit of a misnomer. In fact what we are seeing is the creation of a new post-Roman 'British' culture out of the Romano-British culture of the recent past.

The Latinus stone, along with the other sub-Roman inscriptions of southern Scotland, shows that the local elites were looking south to the wider British-speaking world and consciously aligning themselves with the Britons. In southern Scotland, such assertions were particularly pointed as to the north were the Picts who had never been part of the Empire and for this or other reasons were emphasising their distance from Rome (Fraser 2007). It is tempting to see the contrasting monumental traditions of southern Scotland and Pictland—Latin-inscriptions versus symbol stones—as an epigraphic manifestation of a mutual desire to distinguish themselves from one another. The Cat Stane stands close to the Forth which, at least by the seventh century was considered the southern boundary of the Picts. Across the water in Fife are the most southerly symbol stones (with the example from Princes Street Gardens, Edinburgh, an intriguing outlier).

An important part of this Roman/British cultural package was Christianity, the Imperial religion. The spread of Christianity through southern Scotland arose from elite participation in the Late Roman world, especially with the military in the frontier zone. Christianity had been granted official toleration in 313, and in 380 was declared the only legitimate Imperial religion. From 391 profession of Christianity was a legal requirement for military service. It is likely that Christianisation in northern Britain was in part fuelled by the settlement of Christian veterans, whether locals returning from overseas service, or foreign-born soldiers retiring locally. The importance of Christianity to elite culture in this period is seen throughout the former Empire. Peter Brown has written of the changing attitudes of 'powerful lay Christians' in the late fourth and fifth centuries, to whom 'Christianity had become one of the symbolic forms through which they made their power more present to their inferiors' (Brown 1995, 18). There is perhaps something of this attitude in the fifth-century British inscriptions in which Christianity is still something to be proclaimed. The Trawsfynnyd inscription reads *Porius hic in tumulo iacit homo XPianus fuit*, 'here in the tomb lies Porius, he was a Christian man' (Gresham 1985), a text which implies a local community where such a thing was not yet universal. Similarly the fifth-century memorial to Paulinus from Cynwyl Gaeo, which records in two Latin hexameters that: *Servatur fidaei patri(a)eq(ue) semper amator hic Paulinus iacit cultor pientis(s)imus aequi*, 'Preserver of the faith and always lover of his homeland, here Paulinus lies the most devout supporter of righteousness'. Though more modest in its claims, the Latinus stone—with its unprecedented assertion of faith: *Te dominum laudamus*—belongs here.

One final avenue to be explored in our consideration of the Latinus stone is its possible Irish connections. There is nothing specific about this monument which implies Irish influence: Barrouados could be an Irish name, but is not definitely so, and the use of *nepos* is perhaps best thought of as 'barbarian' rather than specifically Irish. Rather we are talking about the post-Roman epigraphic tradition of western Britain as a whole and the extent to which it was dependent on Irish influence.

There was never any doubt that the use of the Irish ogham script in Wales reflected the presence of Irish-speaking settlers. Yet what has only recently become apparent is the surprising level of Irish involvement in the non-ogham Welsh inscriptions. Recent work by Patrick Sims-Williams (2002, 2003) has revealed the high proportion of diagnostically Irish names among the Celtic personal names in these inscriptions, eg Cunaide, Corbleng. Counting either a diagnostically Irish name or the ogham script as an 'Irish connection', more than two-thirds of the extant 'Group 1' inscriptions in Wales have an 'Irish connection'. The national average—70%—rises even higher in areas of known Irish settlement such as Anglesey and Pembroke and the true proportion of Irish-speakers is likely to be higher still, as some of the Celtic names could be either British or Irish and some Latin names will have been born by Irish-speakers: see the ogham memorials to the Latin-named *Vitalianus* (Nevern), *Similinus* (Clocaenog) and, indeed, *Latinus* (Worthyvale).

Given the extent of Irish settlement in more southerly parts of post-Roman Western Britain, it would not be surprising to find it in Galloway, the part of Britain which is by far the closest to Ireland, but, in fact, there is little evidence of it there. The dense concentration of *sliabh-* place-names in the Rhinns is no longer accepted as a sign of early Gaelic-speaking settlement (Taylor 2007), as had once been proposed (MacQueen 1954; Nicolaisen 1965). A fragment of an incised pillar-stone from Lochnaw in the Rhinns, now in Dumfries Museum, may be the remains of an ogham stone, but this is uncertain (Forsyth 1996, 519-25). The Gaels who brought the Gaelic language to Galloway—as reflected in the many place-names, personal names, and saint dedications of Gaelic-origin (MacQueen 2002; Brooke 1991)—did not settle there until the Viking Age or later. The linguistic and cultural impact of this Medieval Gaelic settlement was strengthened by on-going contacts with north-eastern Ireland and Gaelic-speaking Man throughout the later Medieval and early modern periods (Taylor 2007).

There is ample evidence of links between these same areas in the immediately post-Roman period too. Looking only at the epigraphic evidence there are few ogham inscriptions in north-east Ireland but in the Isle of Man, only 18 miles from Whithorn, there are no less than five early ogham inscriptions (plus a further four from the later period).

Three of these are written in a 'pre-apocope' form of the language, ie the earliest linguistic stage reflected in ogham inscriptions, before the loss of final syllables (one other is certainly post-apocope, a fifth is ambiguous). These three Manx examples are therefore among the earliest of ogham inscriptions and roughly contemporary with the Latinus stone. They are important evidence of the presence of Gaelic speakers in the north, within sight of Whithorn, already in the fifth century. The two inscriptions from Ballaqueeney, Rushen (503/Kerm.1, 504/Kerm.2), are monolingual ogham inscriptions of classic type, but the example from Knock-y-Doonee, Andreas (500/Kerm.6), is a rare northern example of a bi-lingual pillar. Like Whithorn it has a horizontal Latin text, like Chesterholm it pairs horizontality with the *hic iacit* formula. The form of script used at Knock-y-Doonee is a perhaps a little later than that of the Latinus stone (see Tedeschi 2005, 301-2) and the inscription is perhaps late fifth-century, or, at the latest, early sixth-century. Its importance is in demonstrating the interpenetration of the Irish ogham and post-Roman epigraphic traditions in the north already by c.AD 500.

The nature of the sites from which these Manx monuments come may give us further insight into what was going on at fifth-century Whithorn. Both were burial sites with early churches, although, unlike Whithorn, neither became parish churches. The keeill (*cill*, early church site) at Ballaqueeney, in the south of the island, was built on an apparently prehistoric mound with extensive views to the coast. The ogham stones were found during gravel extraction in 1874, reused in lintel graves in the attached rhullick (*reilig*, early burial ground). Pre-Christian activity at the site is further indicated by evidence of cremation (Kelly 1893, 49). The site thus appears to fit the familiar pattern of continuity in family burial places across the pagan/Christian interface.

The name Knock-y-Doonee preserves the early Gaelic ecclesiastical place-name element *domhnach* (< Latin *Dominicum*) (Kneen 1925, 597), although, as at Whithorn, we cannot tell if there was already a church at the site when the monument was erected. The stone was recognised during archaeological excavation of the keeill in 1910. It was standing inverted 'like the headstone of a grave', a few metres outside the keeill in a spot where subsequent excavation uncovered 'certain traces of burial' (Kermode 1911). The inscription, with its *hic iacit* formula, is presumably Christian. The key to the monument's location may be its topographic situation. It occupies a commanding position with extensive, indeed spectacular, views to Ireland, Cumbria and, closest of all, Galloway. The Whithorn peninsula is readily visible. Seventeenth-century records show that Knock-y-Doonee was the location of the day and night watch for the parish (Kneen 1925, 597). It is doubtless this commanding position which attracted the pagan Norse boat burial nearby (Kermode 1927). Knock-y-Doonee serves as a salutory reminder of the vital importance of the seaways to post-Roman western Britain. When the Manx evidence is given due consideration, the Latinus stone no longer seems a distant outlier of an epigraphic tradition centred in west Wales. Instead, its true position in a sea-based geography becomes apparent: Whithorn is close to the former Roman military zone around the Wall, close to Ireland and to Irish settlements in Man, and via Man, linked to the wider western-British world to the south.

Conclusions

The Latinus stone is a lone witness for the fifth century in south-west Scotland. Its testimony is of considerable importance and without it our view of post-Roman Galloway would be markedly different. Previous discussions of post-Roman British epigraphy have tended to emphasise intrusive influence from the Continent (Knight 1992, 1997; Radford 1967; Thomas 1968, 1992a, 1992b, 1997). There is now, however, a growing realisation that the fifth- and sixth-century British epigraphic tradition was not a recent Continental import but a home-grown phenomenon with roots in the Roman period. There is no need to invoke specific Continental influence for details of script or formulae, on the contrary, direct continuity from the Roman period has been demonstrated in both letter-forms and carving technique (Tedeschi 2001; D G Charles-Edwards 2002, 2006; Handley 2001a).

That the Latinus stone is a particularly strong example of this Roman continuity reflects its early date. Indeed it is among the earliest of all the post-Roman inscriptions. In stating the age of the deceased and commemorating the death of young children its text demonstrates a lingering adherence to Roman epigraphic traditions, but its wording is otherwise unusual and does not involve any of the typical formulae. It appears to have been specially composed for the purpose at a point near the beginning of the Christian memorial tradition in Britain, before standard forms were in place. The lettering of the inscription reflects knowledge of both Roman capital and minuscule scripts and familiarity with Roman norms of layout. It is one of the best executed of all the Group 1 inscriptions. Details of its orthography suggest that Latin was a *spoken* language in the area, at least among the elite. The Latinus stone thereby implies a far higher degree of Latinity and literacy in fifth-century Galloway than previous discussions have allowed. A revealing comparison may be made with the somewhat later inscriptions from Kirkmadrine, which come from a scribal, learned, ecclesiastical, milieu (Forsyth 2005). In contrast, the Latinus stone derives from a secular tradition of 'common writing' which originated in the Roman period but, in western Britain, continued for several centuries outside the monastic scriptorium (for which, see D G Charles-Edwards 2006, 2007).

Comparison with other Group 1 inscriptions throws light on the likely archaeological context and social function of the Latinus stone. It will have acted as a burial marker, either of a special grave within a cemetery (like the Catstane) or a single roadside burial (like the grave of *Voteporix* at Castell Dywran). There may or may not have been a church nearby at that time. The stone's location is likely to have been at a significant position in the landscape, perhaps on a territorial boundary, near a secular power centre or beside an important routeway. The monument will have been erected by members of the secular elite, lay Christians in a society where Christianity was not yet the norm. The kinsmen of Barrouados will have been a local landowning family keen to assert their claim to their lands in the most authoritative way open to them, invoking the authority of the old Empire, but also drawing on the more ancient, indigeneous tradition of erecting standing stones. In choosing this form of commemoration, a 'Group 1' inscribed stone, the family were aligning themselves with the nascent post-Roman 'British' culture.

Acknowledgements

This paper is a considerably expanded version of the one delivered at the conference. I am most grateful to the the Friends of the Whithorn Trust for allowing me to publish it here in this form and for their patience during the long wait for the text. I am indebted to the Arts and Humanities Research Council for awarding me a period of research leave during which much of the work on this paper was completed. Finally, I wish to record my gratitude to the following who have provided assistance and insight: Ewan Campbell, Ray Chadburn, the late Gifford Charles-Edwards, Stephen Driscoll, Stephen Gordon, Henry Gough-Cooper, Gilbert Márkus, Tom O'Loughlin, Nigel Ruckley, Ian Scott, Ross Trench-Jellicoe, and Peter Yeoman. What I have made of their input remains, of course, my own responsibility.

References

Allen, J & Anderson J 1903 *The Early Christian Monuments of Scotland*. Society of Antiquaries of Scotland, Edinburgh.

Barnes, R P 1989 *Geology of the Whithorn District*. HMSO, London.

Bartrum, P C (ed and transl) 1966 *Early Welsh Genealogical Tracts*. Univ Wales P, Cardiff.

Bischoff, B 1990 *Latin Paleaography. Antiquity and the Middle Ages*, transl D Ó Cróinín and D Gantz. Cambridge UP, Cambridge.

Bromwich, R (ed and transl) 1961 *Trioedd Ynys Prydein. The Welsh Triads*. Univ Wales P, Cardiff.

Brooke, D 1991 'The Northumbrian settlements in Galloway and Carrick: an historical assessment', *Proc Soc Antiq Scot* 121, 295-327.

Brown, P 1995 *Authority and the sacred. Aspects of the Christianisation of the Roman World*. Cambridge UP, Cambridge.

Charles-Edwards, D G 2002 'The Springmount Bog tablets: their implications for insular palaeography and epigraphy,' *Studia Celtica* 36, 27-46.

Charles-Edwards, D G 2006 The Origin and Development of Insular Geometric Letters, unpublished PhD thesis, University of Wales, Bangor.

Charles-Edwards, D G 2007 'The Palaeography of the inscriptions', *in* Redknap and Lewis, 77-87.

Charles-Edwards, T 1976 'Boundaries in Irish law', *in* Sawyer, P H (ed) *Medieval Settlement. Continuity and Change*, 83-7. London.

Charles-Edwards, T 1995 'Language and Society among the Insular Celts, 400-1000', *in* Green, M (ed) *The Celtic World*, 703-36. Routledge, London.

Collingwood, R G & Wright, R P 1965 *The Roman Inscriptions of Britain. I Inscriptions on stone*. Clarendon, Oxford. (=RIB).

Cowie, T 1978 'Excavations at the Catstane, Midlothian 1977', *Proc Soc Antiq Scot* 109 (1977-78), 166-201.

Craig, D 1992 *The Distribution of Pre-Norman Sculpture in SouthWest Scotland: Provenance, ornament and regional groups*. Unpublished PhD thesis, 4 vols, Durham University.

Craig, D 1997 'Appendix 1. The provenance of the Early Christian inscriptions of Galloway', *in* Hill 1997, 614-20.

Curran, M 1984 *The Antiphonary of Bangor and the Early Irish Monastic Liturgy*. Irish Academic P, Dublin.

Diehl, E 1927 *Inscriptiones Latinae Christianae Veteres*, vol. II, (3 vols, 1925-1931). Berlin.

Ducange, C 1887 *Glossarium Mediae et Infimae latinitatis*, (10 vols 1884-1887) L Favre, Niort.

Duchesne, L 1894 *Fastes episcopaux de l'ancienne Gaul*. Paris.

Edwards, N 2007 *A Corpus of Early Medieval Inscribed Stones and Stone Sculpture in Wales Volume 2 : South-West Wales*. Univ Wales P, Cardiff.

Forsyth, K 1996 *The Ogham Inscriptions of Scotland: An Edited Corpus*. PhD Dissertation, Harvard University, UMI, Ann Arbor Michigan.

Forsyth, K 2005 '*HIC MEMORIA PERPETUA*: the inscribed stones of sub-Roman southern Scotland', *in* Foster, S & Cross, M (eds) *'Able minds and practised hands': Scotland's Early Medieval Sculpture in the 21st Century*, 113-34. Oxbow, Oxford (Society for Medieval Archaeology Monograph series).

Forsyth, K 2008 'The Stones of Deer', *in* Forsyth, K (ed) *Studies on the Book of Deer*, 398-437. Four Courts P, Dublin.

Fraser, J 2007 'The Pictish discovery of Pictishness: constructing an Early Historic Identity', (unpublished paper delivered to the First Millennia Studies Group conference 'Peoples and Tribes in North Britain in the First Millennia – a critical reappraisal', Edinburgh, 5 June 2007).

Gresham A 1985 'Bedd Porius', *Bulletin of the Board of Celtic Studies* 32, 386-92.

Handley, M 1998 'The early medieval inscriptions of Western Britain: function and sociology', in Hill, J & Swan, M (eds) *The Community, the Family and the Saint. Patterns of Power in Early Medieval Europe*, 339-61. Turnhout, Brepols.

Handley, M 2001a 'The origins of Christian commemoration in late antique Britain', *Early Medieval Europe* 10, 177-199.

Handley, M 2001b 'Isidore of Seville and 'Hisperic Latin' in Early Medieval Wales: the epigraphic culture of Llanllyr and Llanddewi-Brefi', *in* Higgitt *et al* (eds), 26-36.

Henry, H T 1912 'The Te Deum', in *The Catholic Encyclopedia*, vol XIV, New York (available on-line at http://www.newadvent.org/cathen/14468c.htm)

Higgit, J 2001 'Form and focus in the Deerhurst dedication inscription', *in* Higgitt *et al* (eds), 89-93.

Higgitt, J, Forsyth, K, & Parsons, D N (eds) 2001 *Roman, Runes and Ogham. Medieval Inscriptions in the Insular World and on the Continent*. Shaun Tyas, Donington.

Hill, P 1997 *Whithorn and St Ninian: The Excavation of a Monastic Town 1984-91*, Sutton/Whithorn Trust, Stroud.

Jackson K H 1953 *Language and History in Early Britain*. Edinburgh UP, Edinburgh.

Kelly, F 1988 *A Guide to Early Irish Law*, Dublin Institute for Advanced Studies.

Kelly, H 1893 'Ballaqueeney cronk, the Clagh Ard or Crosh Ballaqueeney and Cronk Howe Mooar', *Yn Liaor Manninagh* 2.1 (*Proc Isle of Man Nat Hist Antiq Soc*) (1892-3, publ 1901), 47-52.

Kenney, J F 1929 *Sources for the Early History of Ireland. Ecclesiastica.* New York.

Kermode, P M C 1907 *Manx Crosses*, Bemrose, London (reprinted with additional material 1994, Pinkfoot Press, Balgavies, Forfar).

Kermode, P M C, 1911 'Note on the Ogam and Latin inscriptions from the Isle of Man, and a recently found bilingual, in Celtic and Latin', *Proc Soc Antiq Scot* 95 (1910-11), 437-50.

Kermode, P M C 1912 'Cross-slabs recently discovered in the Isle of Man', *Proc Soc Antiq Scot* 96 (1911-12), 53-76.

Kermode, P M C 1927 'Knoc-y-Doonee tumulus, Andreas', *J Manx Museum* 13, 100-01.

Kneen J J 1925 *The Place-names of the Isle of Man*, (published in parts, 1925-9, republished as single volume 1970). Douglas.

Knight, J 1992 'The Early Christian Latin inscriptions of Britain and Gaul: Chronology and context', *in* Edwards, N & Lane, A (eds) *The Early Church in Wales and the West* (Oxbow Monograph 16), 45-50. Oxbow, Oxford.

Knight, J 1997 'Seasoned with salt: Insular Gallic Contacts in the early memorial stones and cross slabs', *in* Dark, K (ed) *External Contacts and the Economy of Late Roman and Post-Roman Britain*, 109-20. Boydell, Woodbridge.

Lowe, C, forthcoming.

M'Kerlie, E M H 1916 *Pilgrim Spots in Galloway*. London.

M'Kerlie, P 1906 *History of the Lands and Their Owners in Galloway, with historical sketches of the district*, new edition, II. Paisley (first edition, 1877, Edinburgh).

Macalister, R A S 1936 'The ancient inscriptions of Kirkmadrine and Whithorn', *Proc Soc Antiq Scot* 70 (1935-6), 315-25.

Macalister, R A S 1945 *Corpus Inscriptionum Insularum Celticarum*, vol 1. Stationery Office, Dublin. (= CIIC).

Macalister, R A S 1949 *Corpus Inscriptionum Insularum Celticarum,* vol 2. Stationery Office, Dublin. (= CIIC).

McManus, D 1991 *A Guide to Ogam* (Maynooth Monographs 4). An Sagart, Maynooth.

MacQueen, J 1954 'Welsh and Gaelic in Galloway', *Trans Dumfriesshire Galloway Nat Hist Antiq Soc* 3rd ser 32, 77-92.

Macqueen, J 1990 *St Nynia*. Polygon, Edinburgh.

MacQueen, J 2002 *Place-Names in the Rhinns of Galloway and Luce Valley*. Stranraer and District Local History Trust, Stranraer.

Nash-Williams, V E 1950 *The Early Christian Monuments of Wales*. University of Wales Press, Cardiff.

Nicolaisen, W F H 1965 'Scottish place-names: 24. *Slew-* and *sliabh*', *Scottish Studies* 9, 91-106.

Niermeyer, J F 1976 *Mediae Latinitatis Lexicon Minus. A Medieval latin-French/English Dictionary*. Leiden.

Okasha, E 1971 *Hand-list of Anglo-Saxon non-runic Inscriptions*. Cambridge UP, Cambridge.

Okasha, E 1993 *Corpus of Early Christian Inscribed Stones of South-west Britain*. Leicester UP, Leicester.

Okasha, E & Forsyth K 2001 *The Early Christian Inscribed Stones of Munster*. Cork UP, Cork.

Radford, C A R 1956 'Excavations at Whithorn (Final Report)', *Trans Dumfriesshire Galloway Nat Hist Archaeol Soc* 3rd ser 34, 131-94.

Radford, C A R 1967 'The early church in Strathclyde and Galloway', *Medieval Archaeology* 11, 105-26.

Radford, C A R & Donaldson, G, 1953 *Whithorn and Kirkmadrine Wigtownshire* Ministry of Works Official Guide book, Edinburgh, H M S O (revised edition = Fisher, I and Tabraham, C J 1984 *Whithorn and the ecclesiastical monuments of Wigtown District*. Edinburgh, H M S O).

Radford, C A R & Donaldson, G 1984 *Whithorn and the ecclesiastical monuments of Wigtown District* (revised edition of Radford and Donaldson 1957 by Fisher, I & Tabraham, C J). HMSO, Edinburgh.

Redknap, M & Lewis, J M 2007 *A Corpus of Early Medieval Inscribed Stones and Stone Sculpture in Wales Volume 1 : South-East Wales and the English Border*. Univ Wales P, Cardiff.

RCAHMS (Royal Commission on the Ancient and Historical Monuments of Scotland) 2007 *St Ninians Cave, Physgill*. Edinburgh.

Ruckley, N A 2004 *Provisional notes on a Magnetic Susceptibility survey of the carved stones at Whithorn Priory Museum, Galloway*. (Unpublished report for Historic Scotland).

Rutherford, A & Ritchie, G 1974 'The Catstane', *Proc Soc Antiq Scot* 105 (1972-4), 183-8.

Sims-Williams, P 2002 'The five languages of Wales in pre-Norman inscriptions', *Cambrian Medieval Celtic Studies* 44, 1-36.

Sims-Williams, P 2003 *The Celtic Inscriptions of Britain: Phonology and Chronology. c400-1200* (Publications of the Philological Society 37). Blackwell, Oxford.

Soutar, A 1949 *A Glossary of Later Latin to 600 AD*. Clarendon, Oxford.

Swift, C 1997 *Ogam Stones and the Earliest Irish Christians*, Maynooth Monographs Series Minor II. Maynooth.

Taylor, S 2007 'Sliabh in Scottish place-names: its meaning and chronology', *J Scottish Name Studs* 1, 99-136.

Tedeschi, C 1995 'Osservazioni sulla paleografia delle iscrizioni britanniche paleocristiane V-VII sec. Contributo allo studio dell'origine delle scritture insulari', *Scrittura e Civiltà* 19, 67-121.

Tedeschi, C 2001 'Some observations on the palaeography of Early Christian inscriptions in Britain', *in* Higgitt *et al* (eds), 16-25.

Tedeschi, C 2005 *Congeries Lapidum. Iscrizioni Britanniche dei secoli V-VII*. Scuola Normale superiore, Pisa.

Thomas, A C 1968 'The evidence from North Britain', *in* Barley, M W & Hanson, R P C (eds) *Christianity in Britain, 300-700*, 93-121. Leicester UP, Leicester.

Thomas, A C 1981 *Christianity in Roman Britain to AD 500*. Batsford, London.

Thomas, A C 1992a *Whithorn's Christian Beginnings* (The First Whithorn Lecture). Friends of the Whithorn Trust, Whithorn.

Thomas, A C 1992b 'The early Christian inscriptions of Southern Scotland', *Glasgow Archaeol J* 17 (1991-2), 1-10.

Thomas, A C 1994 *And Shall These Mute Stones Speak ? Post Roman Inscriptions in Western Britain*. U Wales P, Cardiff.

Thomas, A C 1997 'The Conversions of Scotland' (The John Jamieson Lecture), *Rec Scottish Church Hist Soc* 27, 1-41.

Watt, J M 2001 'William Galloway's Excavations at Whithorn, 1886-1897. Selections from Unpublished Correspondence in the Bute Muniments', *Trans Dumfriesshire Galloway Nat Hist Antiq Soc* 3rd ser 75, 133-49.

Williams, I (ed) 1938 *Canu Aneirin*. Univ Wales P, Cardiff.

Ziegler, S 1994 *Die Sprache der altinschen Ogam-Inschriften*. Göttingen.

Appendix

The following is a list of all Group 1 inscriptions referred to in the text. The name of the principal commemorand is given for reference. Stones marked * are Latin/ogham bi-lingual. Additional references are to the most up-to-date corpora: Tedeschi 2005 and Edwards 2007 or Redknap and Lewis 2007 as appropriate.

Brox, Liddesdale, Roxburghshire (CIIC 514) *Carantius* son of *Cupitianus* (Tedeschi S-2)

Carnsew, Hayle, Cornwall (479/Ok16) *Cunaide* (Tedeschi C-8)

Castell Dwyran, Carmarthenshire (358/138) *Voteporix* * (Tedeschi Gso-8; Edwards CM3 pp.202-6)

Cat Stane, Kirkliston, Mid-Lothian (CIIC 510) *Vetta* (Tedeschi S-3)

Chesterholm (Uindolanda), Northumberland (CIIC 498) *Brigomaglos* (Tedeschi S-1)

Clocaenog, Denbighshire (399/176) *Similinus* * (Tedeschi GN-9)

Cynwyl Gaeo 2, Carmarthenshire (360 /139) *Paulinus* (Tedeschi Gso-7; Edwards CM5 pp208-11)

Eglwys Gymyn 1, Carmarthenshire (362/142) *Avitoria* * (Tedeschi Gso-20; Edwards CM7 pp214-7)

Kirkmadrine, Galloway, *Viventius* and *Florentius* (Tedeschi S-4)

Knock-y-Doonee, Andreas, Isle of Man (500/Kerm.6) *Ammecatos* * (Tedeschi IOM-1)

Llandysul, Cardiganshire (349/121) *Velvoria* (Tedeschi Gso-29; Edwards CD.14)

Llanerfyl, Montgomeryshire (448/370) *Rustica* (Tedeschi Gn-20)

Llangefni, Anglesey (320 /26) *Culidorix* and his wife (Tedeschi Gn-26)

Llansadwrn, Anglesey (323/32) *Saturninus* and his wife (Tedeschi Gn-30)

Llantrisaint (Capel Bronwen), Anglesey (325/33) wife of *Bivatisus* (Tedeschi Gn-6)

Llanymawddwy (Caer Gai), Merionethshire (419/284) *Salvianus* (Tedeschi D-13)

Llywel (Crai), Breconshire (329/42) *Maccutrenos* * (Tedeschi D-3, Redknap and Lewis B41, pp.233-5)

Margam Mountain, Glamorgan (848/229) *Boduoc* (Tedeschi Gse-13; Redknap and Lewis G.77 pp.402-8)

Mathry 1, Pembrokeshire (442/346) *Macudicclus* (Tedeschi Gso-37, Edwards P60 pp380-83)

Nevern 2, Pembrokeshire (445/354) *Vitalianus* * (Tedeschi Gso-39; Edwards P71 pp 392-4)

Penmachno, Caernarfonshire (393/101) *Carausius* (Tedeschi Gn-31)

Trawsfynydd, Merionethshire (420/289) *Porius* (Tedeschi Gn-10; Gresham 1985)

Worthyvale, Cornwall (470/Ok78) *Latinus* * (Tedeschi C-1)

Yarrowkirk, Selkirkshire (CIIC 515) the two sons of *Liberalis* (Tedeschi S-10)

4. Early Christian Cemeteries in south-west Scotland

Dave C Cowley

Introduction

Cemeteries of extended inhumations, often in long cists but also in simple dug graves, are a well-known component of the archaeological record of the mid-1st millennium AD (eg Ashmore 1980; Henshall 1956; Proudfoot 1996; Rees 2002). Ranging in size from just a handful of burials (though single examples have been found) to well over a hundred, the cemeteries are loosely organised, with a generally east to west alignment of the graves. Within the cemeteries, burials arranged in discrete, closely-spaced, clusters are a recurrent feature. The growing numbers of excavated sites with radiocarbon dates indicate a date range between the fourth and the eighth centuries AD (for a recent review of the dating evidence see Rees 2002). This dating, together with a lack of grave goods and a tendency for the body to lie with the head to the west (where this evidence survives), has been taken to indicate burial in a Christian tradition. The known distribution of these cemeteries has a markedly east coast bias (eg Rees 2002, illus 40), with concentrations of sites in East Lothian and Midlothian. This distribution has been largely built up through chance discovery, and to some extent the spread of sites reflects the intensity of archaeological interventions in advance of development in these areas. Extended inhumations in both cists and dug graves are also found under barrows, usually square on plan, but sometimes round, in cemeteries that also contain apparently unelaborated graves (eg Alexander 2005). These too date to the middle centuries of the 1st millennium AD and, while their distribution is also predominately east coast, the vast majority lie to the north of the Forth. The known distribution of barrow cemeteries is largely a product of aerial survey (Maxwell 1983; RCAHMS 1994). Like the distribution of long cists to the south of the Forth, this distribution is biased, but in this case the known sites are skewed towards the arable areas on well-drained soils that are susceptible to cropmarking (see Cowley 2002, and Cowley & Dickson 2007 for discussions of bias in aerial survey data).

The contribution of Aerial survey

Since the inception of intensive and systematic aerial survey in Scotland in the mid-1970s, aerial photography has added to the tally of cemeteries of long cists and dug graves known from excavations (Maxwell 1983). Such sites are identified from characteristic maggot-shaped cropmarks that mark the locations of graves (Figure 1). Indeed, the potential of aerial survey to contribute to the recording of cemeteries extends to medieval graveyards, including both documented and undocumented sites that have gone out of use and been forgotten. Two examples in south-east Scotland have been recorded as cropmarks at Sprouston and Philiphaugh (Smith 1991, 280-3), having been long abandoned and ploughed over. At Sprouston (*ibid*, 280-1) at least 380 graves, the majority of which lie east-north-east to west-south-west, are packed into a roughly rectangular block, in one corner of which there is a possible church, possibly the building documented in the twelfth century (*ibid*, 263). At Philiphaugh, a similar arrangement of graves lies within a ditch-defined enclosure (Figure 2).

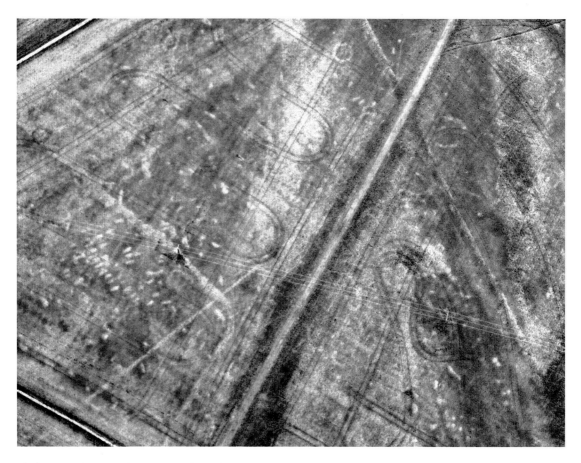

Figure 1: The small 'maggot-shaped' cropmarks recorded on this oblique aerial view at Inveresk, Midlothian (RCAHMS database NT37SW 78), are typical of the long-cist cemeteries that have been recorded in the arable zone during aerial survey (ML3701, © Crown Copyright: RCAHMS).

Figure 2: The cropmarks recorded on this oblique aerial view reveal the closely-packed graves in the medieval cemetery at Philiphaugh, Selkirk (RCAHMS database NT42NE 71), a graveyard that had fallen out of use, been forgotten and eventually ploughed over (B24334, © Crown Copyright: RCAHMS).

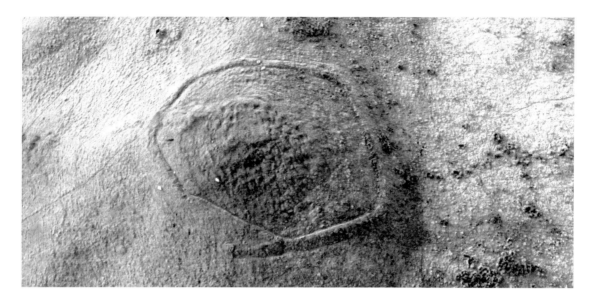

Figure 3: This oblique aerial view shows the enclosure on the summit of Kirk Hill, Ayrshire (RCAHMS database NS20SE 3), and, in the interior, the slight earthworks of grave-pits and what may be the site of a small church, visible as a low subrectangular mound (AY5611, © Crown Copyright: RCAHMS).

A further illustration of the ability of aerial photography to add to the record of lost cemeteries lies on the summit of Kirk Hill, to the north of Dailly in South Ayrshire. This site has been on record since the discovery in about 1795 of a 'stone coffin' on top of the hill (Ordnance Survey, Object Name Book 1856), and there is a local tradition that several oblong mounds on a flat-topped mound within the enclosure covered graves. The remains now survive as low earthworks with a scatter of pits lying within an enclosure. In the past, the numerous roughly rectangular pits in the interior of the enclosure have invited interpretation as tree-throw holes, suggesting that the enclosure was little more than a plantation. However, the aerial photographs (Figure 3) show that these hollows are aligned roughly from east to west, and are more likely to mark the graves of a disused cemetery. In this case, the shallow depressions on the surface suggest that most of the burials are in dug graves covered in earth, rather than cists, formed by the deflation of the soil and decay of the body. However, the earlier reference to a 'stone coffin' suggests that long cists may also be present.

The roughly rectangular mound in the interior of the enclosure is difficult to interpret, but may be the remains of a church, the tradition of which is preserved in the place-name. Thus, Kirk Hill, like Barhobble in Galloway (Cormack 1995, 38), is potentially one of numerous 'lost' church sites scattered across the landscape. The examples cited above illustrate the potential for aerial survey to contribute to their recording, especially through the tell-tale impressions of grave-pits revealed by cropmarking or surviving as low earthworks.

Single burials and earlier traditions

The extensive evidence now available from eastern Scotland can be marshalled to identify some broad features of mid-1st millennium AD cemeteries. These characteristics include extended inhumations found in both stone-lined graves (long cists) and simple dug graves, groups of graves with a broadly east to west alignment, and, to the north of the Forth, a recurrent juxtaposition with square and round barrows (usually ditched). However, there are a few burials in long stone-lined graves, and at least one extended inhumation, that date to the late centuries BC/early centuries AD (eg Ashmore 1980), and this rite clearly has a broader context than the mid-1st millennium AD cemeteries under discussion here. Care should thus be taken not simplistically to extend individual traits to the interpretation of isolated burials, though the body of accumulated evidence does support the interpretation of cemeteries exhibiting these traits as mid-1st millennium AD in date.

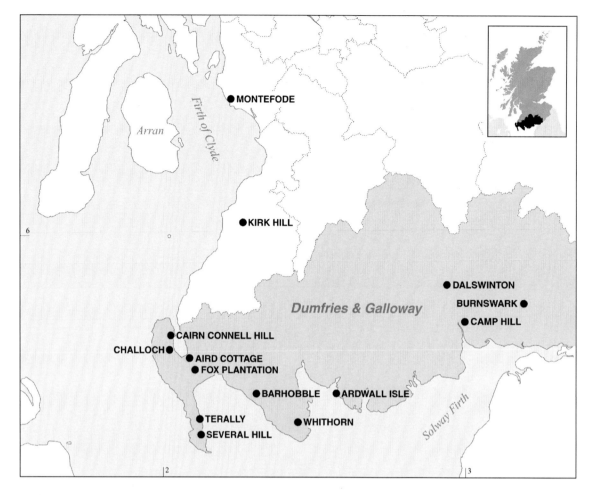

Figure 4: Map of sites in south-west Scotland referred to in the text (© Crown Copyright: RCAHMS).

Allowing for this caveat, there is now a robust body of information on cemeteries of mid-1st millennium AD date derived from excavations and aerial survey in the east of Scotland. What then of the south-west of Scotland?

Cemeteries of the 1st millennium AD in south-west Scotland – the excavated evidence

The thin distribution of excavated cemeteries that date to the mid-1st millennium AD in the south-west of Scotland (Figure 4) is in marked contrast to that found in the east. However, the excavated evidence from Whithorn (Hill 1997) and Montefode (Hatherley forthcoming) are major sources of information, which are supplemented by a handful of other excavated sites across the region.

Whithorn

The substantive burial evidence from Whithorn has been published in detail (Hill 1997), and the following brief review of the earlier burials is drawn from that account. Some 118 graves date to Period I (*c* AD 500 – 730), divided into four distinct phases, between some of which distinctions in grave type are evident (Hill 1997, 70-3). The 'lintel graves' (ie long cists) and 'log-coffin burials' are chronologically distinct and may reflect changes in fashion and/or perhaps the differing status of the individuals interred. The composite plan of all 118 burials from Period I (Figure 5; *ibid,* 71) shows that most of the graves lie roughly east and west, with only a few orientated north-west to south-east. The layout includes rows of graves that clearly referenced each other, less ordered dispositions, and also inter-cutting graves.

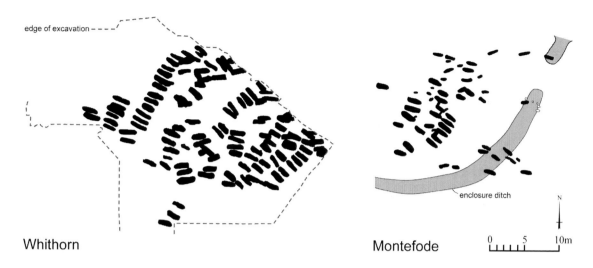

Figure 5: Left - Composite plan of the Period I graves at Whithorn (after Hill 1997, Figure 3.2); Right - Composite plan of the cemetery at Montefode (after Hatherley forthcoming).

Amongst the graves, elaborated or 'special' examples have been identified, which may have been primary or foundation burials, and which provided a focus for further burials. The presence of a small burial enclosure, perhaps measuring little more than 7m in diameter, has been suggested (*ibid*, 87). A circular 'shrine' and a fenced enclosure have also been posited as a focal monument in the Period I graveyard (*ibid*, 91-2, 94). The 'shrines', albeit in fragmentary and uncertain form, remain a feature throughout the phases of Period I, and include one that incorporated a four-post setting of sockets (*ibid*, 103).

Montefode

Excavations in 2003 by Headland Archaeology at Montefode, near Ardrossan, in Ayrshire (Hatherley forthcoming), revealed a cemetery of 60 burials, three of which have been dated to between the mid-6th and mid-7th centuries AD. There are eight long cists, but the majority (49) are simple dug graves (Figure 5). The orientations of burials vary, and the layout of graves includes well-ordered groupings, such as the eight long cists, and looser, less structured arrangements of dug graves. The long cists appear to be earlier than the dug graves. Only a few of the burials lie east and west, with the majority aligned roughly from north-west to south-east. The majority of the burials lie within the interior of an enclosure defined by an arc of ditch set against the south bank of the Montefode Burn. This is probably a later prehistoric settlement which survived in earthwork form when the main group of burials were inserted into its interior, as the majority of the graves clearly avoid a 3-4m wide strip along the inner lip of the ditch, likely to have been occupied by a bank. The further degradation of the enclosure boundary is indicated by the spread of burials cut into the ditch and lying across the area of the putative bank.

The earlier phases of the cemetery occupy the south-east quadrant of the enclosure and the spatial arrangement indicates that, at least on the south-east, the bank and ditch survived in some form when the cemetery was established. However, this does not demonstrate that the cemetery was enclosed, and the spread of graves across the bank and ditch shows a clear disregard for the enclosure boundary, which may even have been a degraded feature when the cemetery was established.

Long cists and dug graves – undated excavated sites

Beyond the modern work at Whithorn and Montefode, there is also a small body of information from excavations undertaken in the late 19th century, the 1950s and the 1960s. For some (eg Terally, below), a date in the mid-1st millennium AD is suggested by analogy, while other sites

Figure 6: Cists at Terally (RCAHMS database NX14SW 8) during excavation in 1956 (photographs R. Livens; © Crown Copyright: RCAHMS).

have been assigned an early Christian date on the basis of their association with what may be an early church (eg Ardwall Isle, below).

The first long cists in the South-west to be excavated, and recognised as such, were those at Terally (Livens 1958, 85-102) and Several Hill (Livens 1960), though other examples may well have been discovered earlier, for example at Curghie (Reid 1959). The cemetery at Terally comprises at least 13 long cists ranged in a rough line along the raised beach, extending to the south-west of a standing stone in the direction of a mound known as the Mote of Terally. The date of the standing stone is not known but, together with the Mote of Terally, it appears to have been a reference point in the layout of the cemetery, enhancing its location on a raised beach at the bottom of a small valley. The cists lie roughly east and west and contained extended inhumations with the head to the west. At least two distinct constructional forms are present: one cist has sides made of two large slabs; the sides of the other were formed of five slightly overlapping slabs (Figure 6).

To these can be added the burials excavated at Ardwall Isle, Camp Hill (Trohoughton) and Barhobble. On Ardwall Isle Thomas (1968) excavated dug graves with extended inhumations lying roughly east and west, with the head at the west. Excavations in the interior of a circular, probably Iron Age, enclosure at Camp Hill, Trohoughton, revealed about 60 dug graves (Simpson & Scott-Elliot 1964). These are aligned either roughly east and west or from north-east to south-west, and clearly postdate a palisade trench, presumably belonging to a phase of the earlier Iron Age settlement. The earliest phase of the burials uncovered at Barhobble underlying the Church may date to the later 1st millennium AD (Cormack 1995), but highlight the potential for such graveyards to add to the corpus of earlier Christian burials.

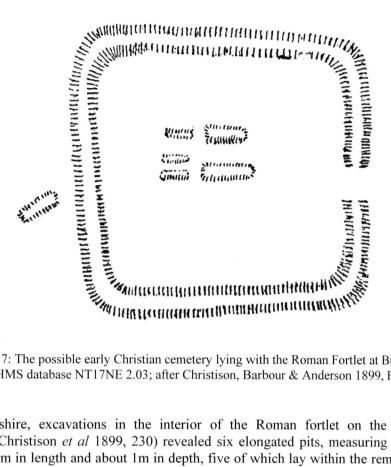

Figure 7: The possible early Christian cemetery lying with the Roman Fortlet at Burnswark (RCAHMS database NT17NE 2.03; after Christison, Barbour & Anderson 1899, Figure 8).

In Dumfriesshire, excavations in the interior of the Roman fortlet on the south side of Burnswark (Christison *et al* 1899, 230) revealed six elongated pits, measuring between about 2.1m and 1.1m in length and about 1m in depth, five of which lay within the remains of a small subsquare enclosure about 7m across (Figure 7). The pits are aligned east and west and the enclosure has been tentatively interpreted as an enclosed Early Christian burial-ground (Jobey 1978; RCAHMS 1997, 181-2). Analogous Early Christian cemeteries have been excavated in Wales (Brassil *et al.* 1991; Lynch & Musson 2004) and at Knockea, in County Limerick, Ireland (O'Kelly 1967; Eogan 1995).

Summary of the excavated evidence

This brief review of the excavated evidence illustrates diversity in both form and context of Early Christian burials in the South-west. However, recurrent traits are also evident, and these can be extended from the excavated sites to create a template against which the coarser-grained evidence from aerial photography can be assessed. For these purposes the key traits are the spatial arrangement of cemeteries, including a tendency to east-west orientation, the clustering of graves, and evidence of both ordered and less-regular layouts. Circular and less-regular enclosed, or otherwise defined areas, such as 'shrines', have been identified at Whithorn, while Burnswark suggests a distinctive form of small enclosed cemetery. The siting of some cemeteries within earlier, presumably derelict enclosures is a characteristic shared by Camp Hill, Montefode and Burnswark, and indicates that in some cases there was a deliberate reuse of such remains by Early Christian communities. Though beyond the scope of this paper, the evidence from Ireland (eg O'Brien 1990; O'Kelly 1967; Seaver 2005) and Wales (above) points to the wider context of the potentially analogous evidence beyond the shores of Scotland.

The evidence from aerial photographs

All the traits of early Christian cemeteries identified above have the potential to be recognised from appropriate aerial photography, formed as they are from features dug into the ground. Indeed, the potential of aerial survey to add to the distribution of cemeteries is firmly established by the results from eastern Scotland (above). In very general terms, aerial

Figure 8: Oblique aerial view of the cropmarks of the late Iron Age rectilinear settlements, round house, possible souterrain and cemetery on Cairn Connell Hill (RCAHMS database NX06NW 41, 42, 43; B72840CN, © Crown Copyright: RCAHMS).

reconnaissance directed to recording plough-levelled and buried monuments as cropmarks in lowland areas carries a greater likelihood of success in areas of well-drained soils, arable cereal cropping and relatively low rainfall (eg Cowley & Dickson 2007, 43-4; Hanson 2005). In practical terms burials are also very small features, especially from 2000 feet, and their discovery also depends on the sharp eyes of the aerial surveyor. Since the west of Scotland is in any case predisposed towards high rainfall, has a relatively small area set to arable and only discrete areas of well-drained soils, the potential contribution of aerial survey might be expected to be minimal.

However, due to unusually dry weather conditions in 1992, when a country-wide drought was at its most extreme in the far south-west of Scotland (Cowley & Brophy 2001), a number of examples were discovered during aerial survey by RCAHMS. These share the basic morphology that has led to the identification of long-cist and dug grave cemeteries in the east of Scotland, and the attributes that have been identified from the excavated cemeteries in the South-west. The cemeteries at Cairn Connell Hill and Challoch are described and illustrated below, followed by examples of possible square burial-enclosures.

Cairn Connell Hill, Kirkcolm

This cemetery is situated on a terrace breaking the north-west flank of Cairn Connell Hill. It enjoys an open aspect across a natural 'amphitheatre' in an arc extending from the north-east around the east across Loch Ryan, and on to the south-east, but has no outlook to the west. The two rectilinear enclosures are visually dominant features on the aerial photographs (Figure 8) and would have first drawn attention to the site from the air. These are settlements dating to the last few centuries BC and first two centuries AD (Cowley 2000, 172-3). Slightly to the east of the enclosures there is a round-house with banana-shaped souterrain (Cowley & Brophy 2001,

67-9), also of later prehistoric date. The graves of the cemetery, which are visible as rather smudgy maggot-like cropmarks, are ranged along the east side of the larger rectilinear enclosure, in the gap between the two enclosures and around the unenclosed round-house and souterrain. Between 35 and 40 are visible, aligned from east-north-east to west-south-west, though slight variations from this trend may also be present. Another noteworthy component is a small ring-ditch measuring about 6.5m in diameter, which lies immediately to the south of the round-house and souterrain. This feature may be the bedding trench of a timber round-house, like those inside the larger rectilinear enclosure, but the identification of the small circular 'shrines' at Whithorn presents itself as a possible alternative interpretation.

The nature of the evidence, essentially a plan view of remains that would certainly be more complex if excavated, places some limitations on the interpretation of possible sequences of activity. The disposition of graves in a row immediately to the east of the boundary of the larger settlement suggests that its ditch informed the layout of the cemetery. However, by the middle centuries of the 1st millennium AD, it is likely that the two rectilinear enclosures, the round house and the souterrain were all derelict. Situated on a relatively sheltered terrace, the cemetery nonetheless would have been on the skyline from across much of the natural 'amphitheatre' to the east, in which the village of Kirkcolm now nestles.

Challoch, Leswalt

The greater part of the cemetery at Challoch is ranged along a narrow, but pronounced, terrace breaking a steep north-east facing hillside to the south of Leswalt village. It thus has an extensive outlook in an arc from the north-west, around the north and north-east to due east, where the hillside truncates the view. The cemetery commands extensive views across the greater part of the valley of the Sole Burn, though its location on a hillside does not lend itself to easy identification from any distance. Cairn Connell Hill lies just out of sight to the north. The cropmarks at Challoch include maggot-shaped grave-pits, two small ring-ditches, and what may be an irregular enclosure; some of the graves lie within the enclosure (Figure 9).

There are in the order of 100 graves, of which about 70 lie on the narrow terrace, with a further 30 or so slightly further up the hill on a low rise occupied by the irregular enclosure. This clustering, however, may be an artefact of local variations in the responsiveness of the crop rather than the layout of the cemetery; the dark areas on the photographs correspond to deeper soils which are less sensitive to cropmarking than the shallower soils in the light areas. That said, the disposition of the cropmarked features along the pronounced terrace suggests that here, at least, the visible features may well correspond with the true extent and plan of the cemetery. The graves are aligned from east to west, clustering into discrete blocks of strictly ordered rows interspersed with somewhat ragged groups.

At the west end of the terrace there is a small ring-ditch, measuring about 5m in diameter, within which there are several 'blobs' which may be graves. A similar ring-ditch lies about 50m to the south, and in both cases the broadness of the ditch relative to the size of the interior invites comparison with small barrows usually assumed to be prehistoric in date (eg Cowley & Brophy 2001, 59-60). However, the juxtaposition of the ring-ditch and graves also brings to mind the arrangement of burials and 'shrine' at Whithorn. The irregular enclosure, which is open on the south, either because this sector has not registered as a cropmark, or did not exist, is unusual for the south-west of Scotland and does not sit comfortably in the cannon of later prehistoric settlement enclosures. A handful of graves lie within it and there is a block of closely-spaced, regularly aligned graves just outside its perimeter on the east. The inter-relation of enclosure and graves cannot, however, be judged from the aerial photography alone.

Square Burial Enclosures

The identification of what may be a small early Christian enclosed burial ground at Burnswark (above, Figure 7; Jobey 1978) provides a possible analogy for three sites found in the aerial

Figure 9: Oblique aerial view of the cropmarks of the cemetery at Challoch
(RCAHMS database NX06SW 25, 26; B79762, © Crown Copyright: RCAHMS).

photographic record. Rectilinear enclosures are a recurrent theme in the archaeology of the south-west and include later prehistoric settlements (RCAHMS 1997, 154-5; Cowley 2000, 172-3; Cowley & Brophy 2001, 61) and what may be yards and gardens in medieval or post-medieval farmsteads. The three identified here, however, are marked out by their relatively small size and morphological uniformity, which contrasts with the consistently larger later prehistoric settlement enclosures.

The first, at Aird Cottage (Figure 10, A), is a squarish enclosure measuring about 10m across within a ditch about 2m in breadth. In the interior there are some poorly defined elongated pits, aligned roughly from east to west, which might be graves. The second, lying on a broad terrace near Fox Plantation and overlooking the Soulseat Burn, is a rectangular enclosure measuring about 10m by 8m internally (Figure 10, B). In this case, there is no sign of grave-pits, though there are several circular pits outside the enclosure. Finally, at Dalswinton (Figure 10, C), there is a rectangular enclosure, which measures about 14m by 12m internally; while there are indefinite small marks in its interior, these cannot be identified as graves with any certainty. These three sites are oddities amongst the rectilinear and square enclosures in the South-west, and do not fit within the group of recognisably later prehistoric rectilinear settlements. The putatively Early Christian enclosed cemetery at Burnswark provides the only close analogy

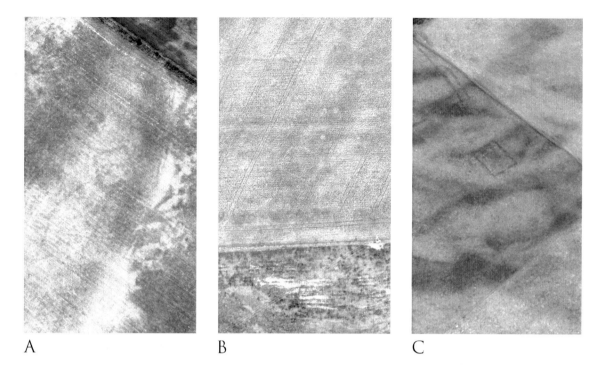

A   B   C

Figure 10: Oblique aerial views of possible square burial enclosures at Aird Cottage (A – RCAHMS database NX06SE 93; DF2135), Fox Plantation (B – RCAHMS database NX15NW 15; WG861) and Dalswinton (C – RCAHMS database NX98SW 48; C0004; all three images © Crown Copyright: RCAHMS).

from the excavation record, albeit on the basis of fairly basic attributes. This analogy, and their distinctiveness, suggest that they would repay further investigation in any search for early Christian cemeteries.

Early Christian cemeteries in south-west Scotland

Two certain examples of cemeteries of long cists or dug graves have been identified from aerial photographs in Galloway. On the basis of the extensive data from the east of Scotland, Whithorn and Montefode, these can be identified as Christian cemeteries dating to the middle centuries of the 1st millennium AD. In particular, the similarities in layout of the earliest phases of the Whithorn cemetery suggest that Cairn Connell Hill and Challoch too are Early Christian in date.

The spatial arrangement of graves, in both discrete tight groups and looser scatters, and the roughly east to west alignment of most burials, are recurrent themes shared with sites in the east. Whithorn and Montefode both indicate that this patterning reflects both the development of the cemeteries over time and variation in the status of individual inhumations, from primary 'foundation burials' around which other 'high status' burials may cluster to looser scatters of less ordered burials. The evidence from Whithorn and Montefode indicates that stone-lined long-cists may be earlier in date (eg sixth/seventh centuries AD) than the dug graves (eg seventh/eighth centuries AD), though the difference between these burial types is not discernable from aerial photographic evidence. The Whithorn 'shrines', and their potential analogues in the aerial photographs at Cairn Connell Hill and Challoch, may be a peculiarity to the South-west, but they also stand as a challenge to the interpretation of small enclosures or ring-ditches in long cist cemeteries elsewhere.

The positions of the Cairn Connell Hill and Challoch cemeteries show a shared concern with outlook, occupying locations towards the fringes of topographically defined units of ground over which they enjoy extensive views. This possible relationship with naturally bounded blocks of land invites an interpretation of the cemeteries as reflecting a community and its territory. This may also be the case at Terally, where the cemetery sits on a raised beach at the centre of a small bay with an open outlook across much of a small valley on the landward side – again a distinct topographic unit. Thus, these cemeteries may provide a clue to the organisation of the earliest Christian populations in The Rhins of Galloway. The topographic location of the cemeteries at Cairn Connell Hill and Challoch on hillsides set above a medieval parish church and village on the valley floor may be coincidental, but is distinctive enough to merit comment. The juxtaposition of the possibly prehistoric standing stone and the long cists at Terally may reflect the appropriation of older monuments by a Christian community. This too is a possible explanation for the ring-ditch features at Challoch (above), which may equally be prehistoric barrows as components of the Christian cemetery. Indeed, this may be part of a wider process which saw new burial rites introduced, alongside the development or assimilation of older burial customs or the appropriation of earlier monuments (eg Barclay 1983; O'Brien 1990, 1999). The reuse of the interiors of derelict enclosures at Montefode, Camp Hill (Trohoughton) and Burnswark, and the juxtaposition of the cemetery with late Iron Age settlement enclosures at Cairn Connell Hill, may be a further expression of a desire to appropriate earlier monuments. However, Challoch demonstrates that this was not a universal trait.

Conclusions

Sites identified from aerial photography have expanded the evidence for the earliest Christian cemeteries in Galloway, suggesting them to be widely dispersed across the landscape, probably reflecting the disposition of local communities, in which the origins of later parish units may lie. These sites help to fill out the broader context for Whithorn as a focus for Early Christian communities in the South-west. Looking beyond Galloway, the growing evidence for Early Christian burials from both south-west Scotland and Ireland is a considerable enhancement to the available information in considering the wider context of the emergence of Christianity in the Irish Sea area.

Acknowledgments

I am grateful to Ian Doyle for his kindness in sending me a bulging envelope of papers on recent Irish excavations; to Strat Halliday for discussing many of these sites, commenting on the text and drawing my attention to Kirk Hill; to Candy Hatherley for making the Montefode material available in advance of publication, and to Jack Stevenson for editing the text. My thanks also to Kevin Macleod for preparing figures 4 and 5.

References

Alexander, D 2005 'Redcastle, Lunan Bay, Angus: the excavation of an Iron Age timber-lined souterrain and a Pictish barrow cemetery', *Proc Soc Antiq Scot* 135, 41-118.

Ashmore, P 1980 'Low cairns, long cists and symbol stones', *Proc Soc Antiq Scot* 110 (1978-80), 346-55.

Barclay, G J 1983 'Sites of the third millennium bc to the first millennium ad at North Mains, Strathallan, Perthshire', *Proc Soc Antiq Scot* 113, 122-281.

Brassil, K S, Owen, W G, & Britnell, W J 1991 'Prehistoric and early medieval cemeteries at Tandderwen, near Denbigh, Clwyd', *Archaeological J* 148, 46-97.

Christison, D, Barbour, J, & Anderson, J 1899 'Account of the Excavation of the Camps and earthworks at Birrenswark Hill, in Annandale, undertaken by the Society in 1898', *Proc Soc Antiq Scot* 33 (1898-9), 198-249.

Cormack, W F 1995 'Barhobble, Mochrum Excavation of a forgotten church site in Galloway', *Trans Dumfriesshire Galloway Nat Hist Antiq Soc* 3rd series, 70, 5-106.

Cowley, D C 2000 'Site morphology and regional variation in the later prehistoric settlement of south-west Scotland', *in* Harding, J & Johnston, R (eds) *Northern Pasts – Interpretations of the Later Prehistory of Northern England and Southern Scotland*, 167-76. Oxford (=Brit Archaeol Rep, Brit Ser 302).

Cowley, D C 2002 'A case study in the analysis of patterns of aerial reconnaissance in a lowland area of southwest Scotland' *Archaeological Prospection* 9, issue 4, 255-65.

Cowley, D C & Brophy, K 2001 'The impact of aerial photography across the lowlands of south-west Scotland', *Trans Dumfriesshire Galloway Nat Hist Antiq Soc* 3rd series, 75 (2001), 47-72.

Cowley, D C & Dickson, A L 2007 'Clays and 'difficult' soils in eastern and southern Scotland: dealing with the gaps', *in* Mills, J & Palmer, R (eds) *Populating Clay Landscapes*, 43-54. Tempus, Stroud.

Eogan, J 1995 'Knockea, Co. Limerick – A unique Early Christian ritual monument', *Trowel (The Journal of the Archaeological Society University College Dublin)* VI, 18-22.

Hanson, W S 2005 'Sun, sand and see: creating bias in the archaeological record, *in* Brophy, K & Cowley, D C (eds) *From the Air – understanding Aerial Archaeology*, 73-85. Tempus, Stroud.

Hatherley, C forthcoming 'Into the west: excavation of an Early Christian cemetery at Montefode, Ardrossan', *Proc Soc Antiq Scot.*

Henshall, A S 1956 'A Long Cist Cemetery at Parkburn Sand Pit, Lasswade, Midlothian' *Proc. Soc. Antiq. Scot.* 89 (1955-56), 252-83.

Hill, P 1997 *Whithorn and St Ninian: The Excavation of a Monastic Town 1984-91*, Sutton/Whithorn Trust, Stroud.

Jobey, G 1978 'Burnswark Hill, Dumfriesshire', *Trans Dumfriesshire Galloway Nat Hist Antiq Soc* 3rd series, 53, 57-104.

Livens, R G 1958 'Excavations at Terally (Wigtownshire), 1956', *Trans Dumfriesshire Galloway Nat Hist Antiq Soc* 3rd series, 35 (1956-57), 85-102.

Livens, R G 1960 'Several, Drummore, Kirkmaiden', *Discovery and Excavation Scotland 1960*, Council for British Archaeology, 41.

Lynch, F & Musson, C 2004 'A prehistoric and early medieval complex at Llandegai, near Bangor, North Wales', *Archaeologia Cambrensis* 150 (2001), 17-142.

Maxwell, G S 1983 'Recent aerial survey in Scotland', *in* Maxwell, G S (ed) *The impact of aerial reconnaissance on archaeology*, Council for British Archaeology Research Report No 49, 27-40.

O'Brien, E 1990 'Iron Age Burial Practices in Leinster: Continuity and Change', *Emania – Bulletin of the Navan Research Group*, No 7, 37-42.

O'Brien, E 1999 *Post-Roman Britain to Anglo-Saxon England: Burial Practices Reviewed.* Oxford (=Brit Archaeol Rep, Brit Ser 289).

O'Kelly, M.J. 1967 'Knockea, Co Limerick', in Rynne, E (ed) *North Munster Studies – Essays in commemoration of Monsignor Michael Moloney*, The Thomond Archaeological Society, 72-101.

Proudfoot, E 1996 'Excavations at the long cist cemetery on the Hallow Hill, St Andrews, Fife', 1975-7, *Proc Soc Antiq Scot* 126, 387-454.

RCAHMS (Royal Commission on the Ancient and Historical Monuments of Scotland) 1994 *South-east Perth an archaeological landscape*, HMSO.

RCAHMS (Royal Commission on the Ancient and Historical Monuments of Scotland) 1997 *Eastern Dumfriesshire – an archaeological landscape*, TSO.

Rees, A R 2002 'A first millennium AD cemetery, rectangular Bronze Age structure and late prehistoric settlement at Thornybank, Midlothian', *Proc Soc Antiq Scot* 132, 313-55.

Reid, R C 1959 'The Ventidius Stone, Kirkmaiden', *Trans Dumfriesshire Galloway Nat Hist Antiq Soc* 3rd series, 36 (1957-58), 184-5.

Seaver, M 2005 'Run of the Mill? Excavation of an early medieval site at Raystown, Co. Meath', *Archaeology Ireland*, Winter 2005, 9-12.

Simpson, D D A & Scott-Elliot, J 1964 'Excavation at Camp Hill, Trohoughton, Dumfries', *Trans Dumfriesshire Galloway Nat Hist Antiq Soc* 3rd series, 41 (1962-63), 125-34.

Smith, I M 1991 'Sprouston, Roxburghshire: an early Anglian centre of the eastern Tweed Basin', *Proc Soc Antiq Scot* 121, 261-94.

Thomas, C 1968 'An Early Christian Cemetery and Chapel on Ardwall Isle, Kirkcudbright', *Medieval Archaeology*, 11 (1967), 127-88.

5. Christianity in northern Britain in the late-Roman period: a critical assessment

Mike McCarthy

Since Radford's rather pessimistic presidential address delivered to the Society for Medieval Archaeology in 1970 there has been a marked increase in research on the theme of Christianity in Roman Britain (Radford 1971; Thomas, 1971; 1981). It is not my intention to review these developments (see, for example, Frend 1992, 1994, 1996, 2003; Mawer 1995; Painter 1994; Petts 2003; Thomas 1992; 1994; 1998; Watts 1991; 1998; Wood 2004), but rather to assess the alleged evidence for the practice of Christianity in north Britain in the fourth century AD.

The evidence

Of the various categories of enquiry that archaeologists might seek to address, religion is one of the most problematic. Whether Christian or pagan, worship and ritual demand a belief in the efficacy of certain 'powers transcending human life', as the late Grahame Clark put it (Clark 1957, 234). Unfortunately, such things do not always translate readily into concrete terms such as ritual buildings or equipment, as is apparent throughout much of the Celtic world. In the case of Christianity, for many generations after the death of Jesus, believers seem to have been content with using private houses for devotional purposes. We can see this in the first century, in the Acts of the Apostles and the Pauline correspondence, but it was still true in third century Dura Europos on the Tigris at one end of the Empire, and in fourth-century Britain at Lullingstone, Kent at the other. It was equally true of Christianity's parent belief system, Judaism, and the growth of the synagogue.

For over 300 years after Christ's death, and long after Constantine's conversion, the formats of liturgies, and ritual, as well as the design and layout of churches, were in a state of flux, and it took time before the cross, that ubiquitous symbol of Christ, was universally adopted. Whereas in the first instance what was important was the act of worship itself, what *became* important in the fourth century was both the underlying theology and the need for buildings containing specific spaces for the performance of ritual related to the theology. The fourth century can, therefore, be seen as a transitional period in which the church learned to adapt existing buildings or an existing architecture to its own purposes. It is in this that the archaeological record is ambivalent when it comes to separating Christian from non-Christian or non-religious military functions. In Britain, where remains survive only at the lowest-course or sub-surface foundation level, distinguishing between a church and some other function is problematical, as the different interpretations put on the Silchester 'church' show very clearly (Frere 1975; King 1983). Furthermore, in the fields of art and the semiotics of dress and personal ornament, images, symbols or phrases that could easily have a simple secular or decorative intent could also be adopted within a repertoire of religious iconography. In other words, considerable caution is needed when it comes to interpreting archaeological remains and artefacts as

Christian. There is more than one way of interpreting rectangular structures with apses, or images comprising two lines intersecting at an angle of around 90 degrees.

All this raises the question of whether we can ever expect to be able to do much more than speculate on the identification of Christian communities in a remote northern province before the church had adopted architectural and liturgical conventions. I have taken as my starting point Table 1, which brings together a variety of materials collected and mostly accepted by scholars and cited as evidence, or possible evidence, for Christian worship in the northern counties of England and Dumfries and Galloway during the fourth century AD. The evidence takes the form of portable objects, structural remains including tombstones and graves, and texts.

TABLE 1

Possible evidence for Christianity in northern Britain in the fourth to early fifth centuries

Place	Item	Comment	Reference
Cumbria			
Carlisle	Tombstone	Papias & '*plus minus*'	RIB 955; Toynbee 1953; Handley 2001, 184
Birdoswald	?Church	Modern excavation	Burnham 2000, 391.
Bannavem Taburniae - ?Birdoswald	Priest & deacon	St Patrick, *Confessio*	Hood 1978; Thomas 1981, 310-14
Brough under Stainmore	Ring	*Chi-rho*	RIB 2422.81; Mawer 1995, 78
Maryport	Tombstone	*Chi-rho*	RIB 856
Maryport	Tombstone	Quality of epigraphy	RIB 862; Forsyth 2005, 116
Maryport	Tombstone	Quality of epigraphy	RIB 863; Forsyth 2005, 116
Brougham	Tombstone	'*plus minus*'	RIB 787; Fitzpatrick 2004
Brougham	Tombstone	'*titulo posuit*'	RIB 786; Handley 2001
Old Penrith	Tombstone	'*titulum posuit*'	RIB 934; Handley 2001, 181
Old Carlisle	Tombstone	Quality of epigraphy	RIB 908; Forsyth 2005, 116
Ireby	Lead tank	Decorated with circles	Guy 1981; Watts 1988
Northumbria			
Bywell	Silver beaker	Inscription – doubtful Christian	RIB 2414.32; Mawer 1995, 14-15
Carrawburgh	Glass vessel	?Fish	Mawer 1995, 31
Cawfields	Tombstone	'*titulum posuit*'	RIB 1667; Handley 2001, 184
Chesters	Glass vessel	Fish; *a + m*	RIB 2419.62; Mawer 1995, 30
Chesters	Jet ring	*Chi-rho*	RIB 2422.8; Mawer 1995, 75-6
Vindolanda	Tombstone	Brigomaglos	RIB 1722; CIIC 498
Vindolanda	'Small portable altar-like stone'	*Chi-rho*	Burnham 2000, 390
Vindolanda	Church	Modern excavation	Birley *et al* 1999
Corbridge	?Church	1912 excavation – *schola*	Forster & Knowles 1913
Corbridge	Glass vessel	Fish; letters incl *m*	RIB 2419.61; Mawer 1995, 30-1
Corbridge	Gold ring	Inscription Aemilia	RIB 2422.1; Mawer 1995, 68
Corbridge	Silver bowl	*Chi-rho*	RIB 2414.39; Mawer 1995, 17-18

Housesteads	?Church	Seen in 19th century	Crow 1995, 95, 97
Tyne and Wear			
Newcastle	Lamp	? doubtful *chi-rho*	Mawer 1995, 8
S Shields	?Church + altar	19th cent excavation	Bidwell & Speak 1994, 103-4
North Yorkshire			
York	Bishop	Council of Arles	
York	Tile (tegula)	*Chi-rho*	RIB 2491.160
York	Gold plate	Inscription – ? Christian	RIB 706; Mawer 1995, 84
York	Bone plaque	Inscription	RIB 2441.11; Mawer 1995, 86-7
York	*c* 50 burials	Gypsum – details variable	Ramm 1971, 193-4; RCHM 1962, 67-110
Catterick	Tombstone		Wright 1967, no.8; Handley 2001, 181
Beadlam	Strap end	Fish	Mawer 1995, 63
Durham			
Binchester	Pot	?*chi-rho* and *a+m*	RIB 2503.551; Mawer 1995, 35-6
West Yorkshire			
Wetherby	At least 11 burials	Lack of grave goods	Faull & Moorhouse 1981: 145
Malton	Burial	Traces gypsum, coin Constans	Philpott 1991, 312
Castleford	Burial	Gypsum	Philpott 1991, 312; Ramm 1971, 195
Glass Houghton	Burial	Gypsum E-W orientation	Faull & Moorhouse 1981: 157.
Hunslet	Burial	Gypsum N-S orientation, grave goods	Faull & Moorhouse 1981: 157.
Birkin	Burial	Possible gypsum	Ramm 1971, 195
Pollington	Burial	Gypsum, E-W orientation, stone coffin	Ramm 1971: 195
Dumfriesshire and Galloway			
Whithorn	Memorial stone	Latinus	Thomas 1981, 283-5; 1992, 1998, 104-14; Craig 1997, 615-6; Hill 2001
Whithorn	Bishop	Ninian	Bede *HE* III, 4

Portable artefacts

Portable items are a contentious category of evidence representing an optimistic and largely insecure foundation on which to build a case for the practice of Christianity. Whilst a Christian interpretation of the images on some objects (both the York plaques; the Chesters jet ring; the glass from Chesters, Corbridge and Carrawburgh) is acceptable, they are not evidence of Christian worship at or near their findspots. The reason is straightforward. By definition, portable items can be easily transported, so that jewellery, vessels or dress attachments can be imported from almost anywhere before being lost or discarded. Moreover, in some cases, such as the Beadlam strap-end, we cannot be sure that the imagery employed was 'certainly and unambiguously Christian' and intended only for a Christian audience (Elsner 2003, 114-5). After all, as Ward-Perkins noted long ago, craftsmen made objects with no interest or concern with meaning provided they sold. 'Meaning' was something added by the purchaser (Ward

Perkins 1978). Another instance is the Ireby lead tank, currently an outlier of a group of lead tanks found mostly in East Anglia, the Midlands and the south. It is not only the smallest and shallowest of its type, but unlike some of the others it bears no unambiguously Christian symbols. Richmond (1945) thought it was a vat, but both Guy (1981, 275) and Watts (1991, 163-8) argued that the circles may represent the cosmos, time, the world and God. If they are right, a function in connection with either baptism or the ritual of foot washing is certainly as plausible as a domestic or agricultural use.

If 'small finds' are an unreliable guide to Christian worship, we should not throw the baby out with the bathwater, as it were. Occasionally a Christian symbol may have some significance in a local context. The graffiti on a pot found at Binchester, County Durham, was dismissed by Mawer, but is upheld by the excavator, Dr. Rick Jones, who considers the pot to be a votive deposit in the mid-fourth-century foundation of the *praetorium*.

Structural remains

Tombstones

Unlike portable finds, tombstones are rarely found very far from their original location, and when they are, they were often used as building material or hardcore. Thus, tombstones tend to reflect activities or beliefs very close to their findspots.

At Maryport, a lost stone with dimensions of 6 x 12 inches (*c*15 x 30cm) bearing a *chi-rho* (RIB 856) may be a broken tombstone, and along with the Latinus stone at Whithorn, is one of the few unambiguously Christian items from northern Britain. Another frequently cited stone commemorates Flavius Antigonus Papias (RIB 955), and was found marking one of many graves forming a linear cemetery on the southern approach to Carlisle (Ferguson 1893, 369-70; Charlesworth 1978, 124). It bears the words '*dis manibus*' and '*plus minus*', the latter being the main reason why it is believed to be Christian. Although the Christian credentials of this stone have been questioned (Toynbee 1953), it is nevertheless widely regarded as such, not least because, as RIB notes, it also includes the possibly Christian sentiment, 'gave back to the Fates his soul lent for that extent of time', whilst Papias's Greek origin shows that he came from an area that had long been Christianised.

The cemetery at Brougham, east of Penrith, Cumbria, excavated by the late Dorothy Charlesworth in the 1960s (Cool 2004), contained many cremations and inhumations as well as a number of tombstones, two of which may be regarded as Christian. The cemetery, including all the tombstones, is attributed to the third century, on the basis of pottery and other items found associated with the graves. However, Handley has suggested that RIB 786, found in the nineteenth century towards the eastern end of the cemetery, can be re-dated to the fourth century on the grounds that it combines the often pagan formula *dis manibus* with the frequently Christian phrase *titulum posuit* (Handley 2001, 181-4). As he notes, there are hundreds of Christian inscriptions with both these formulae in Gaul, Spain, North Africa and Italy.

The Christian credentials of another Brougham tombstone (RIB 787) have also been questioned (Fitzpatrick 2004, 427, 435). In this case the stone was found incorporated in the masonry of the adjacent Brougham castle in 1760, but its original find spot is unknown. As with Carlisle RIB 955, the stone bears the words *dis manibus* and *plus minus*, but Fitzpatrick rejected a fourth-century date and a Christian affiliation on the grounds that the excavated graves lie within the bracket AD 220-310. This is wholly unconvincing in the light of Handley's discussion on formulae elsewhere in the Western Roman Empire (2001, 181-4). It also lacks conviction in the context of Brougham given our ignorance as to its original location, as well as the near certainty of fourth-century occupation implied by the presence of pottery, coins and seven long cists incorporating some broken Roman tombstones of late or sub-Roman date (Shotter 2000, 32; Wilmott 2004, 8; Cool 2004, 36-8).

At Vindolanda, a tombstone to Brigomaglos (RIB 1772) includes the word *iacit,* which is usually thought of as sub- or post-Roman in date. However, as Handley has argued, *hic iacets* are commonly used in western Europe and north Africa from the mid fourth century on, so that a late-Roman attribution might now be preferred (Handley 2001, 185-8; Swift 1997, 103). The quality of the inscription is also very crude, a characteristic that led Forsyth to note that stones with even cruder lettering from Maryport and Old Carlisle may also be attributable to the fourth century (RIB 862-3; RIB 908; Forsyth 2005, 116).

In addition to the stones mentioned above, Handley (2001, 181-2) notes other tombstones with the combination of *dis manibus* and *titulum posuit* from Old Penrith, Cumbria, and Cawfields on Hadrian's Wall (RIB 934; RIB 1667), as well as Catterick (Wright 1967 no 8) and York (RIB 689), whilst two more from York (RIB 672, 677) bearing the word *memoriae* may also be admitted to the category of possible evidence. Charles Thomas has also drawn attention to Birley's comment that RIB 1828, a 'presumably third century' tombstone of Aurelia from Salonae in Dalmatia, found at Carvoran on Hadrian's Wall, contains the phrase '*sine ulla macula*' – without any blemish. This too can be found on some Christian tombstones (Thomas 1971, 11).

Burials

No late Roman burials with unambiguously Christian associations have been excavated in northern Britain. More Roman burials are known from York than most other places, but these are chiefly eighteenth- to early twentieth-century discoveries. The records are extremely uneven and varied in the detail they contain, but they show that at least 49 were encased in, or associated with, gypsum. Whilst the practice of using gypsum for preserving bodies prior to the resurrection was adopted by Christians (Green 1977; Sparey-Green 2003), the idea that this was an exclusively Christian habit is no longer accepted by many scholars, and some argue that the distinction between Christian and non-Christian burials is not necessarily clear cut. (Philpott 1991, 90-6). For the present it is sufficient to note that at York at least 31 such burials were found in the cemetery around the Railway Station (RCHM 1962; Ramm 1971, 193-4), which is close to the postulated site of the governor's *praetorium* where Constantine is likely to have been accommodated (Bidwell 2006). It may have been a place, therefore, with which Christians might wish to have been associated in death.

Other burials have also been claimed as possibly Christian, including a group at Wetherby (Faull 1977, 26-30; Faull and Moorhouse, 1981, 145), but none contain unambiguously Christian features.

Churches

Churches that can be attributed to the fourth century are known from various parts of the Roman Empire (Krautheimer 1965), but in Britain remains are generally scrappy and their interpretation is, in most instances, questionable. The provincial capital of York, the place where Constantine was elevated to the imperial throne, is known to have had a bishop, which means that we can be fairly confident that the city housed at least one, if not more, churches. However, despite a long history of antiquarian and archaeological endeavour, nothing has emerged so far that can be interpreted as a late Roman church using the models available from elsewhere in the Empire (RCHM 1962; Ottaway 1993, 107-8).

Outside York there are a number of possible sites within the Hadrian's Wall military zone. At the fort of Vindolanda, the *praetorium* apparently functioned during the mid to later fourth century. In the courtyard, on top of about 20cm of soil overlying the latest surface, lay the foundations of a small east-west oriented building with a western apse. The 'nave' abutted the east range of the *praetorium,* and a date of about AD 400 was suggested (Birley *et al* 1999). The interpretation of the building as a church was made largely on the basis of the plan, but it is not the only indicator of Christianity at Vindolanda because a 'small portable altar-like stone' with an incised *chi-rho,* attributed on stylistic grounds to around AD 500-550, has been recovered from the surface of a sub-Roman structure overlying the western ditch (Burnham 2000, 390), and there is the stone dedicated to Brigomaglos.

Other sites include Housesteads, where a photograph of Bosanquet's 1898 excavations shows a structure near the north wall apparently with a western apse and a stone flagged floor. It is said to overlie a layer of black soil, which must itself have covered the remains of barracks and intervallum road. The sequence is not unlike that at Vindolanda, but too little of the plan and stratigraphic relationships are known for us to have any confidence in the interpretation. Nevertheless, it is clearly a late Roman, if not a post-fourth-century, structure, and cannot at present be eliminated as a possible church (Crow 1995, 95-7).

Similarly, at Birdoswald work in the north-western corner of the fort revealed a small stone building with a western apse constructed in the late fourth century, but no other details are available largely because the latest deposits had been severely damaged by later activity (Burnham 2000, 391). However, given its date and the presence of an apse, it may also be considered as a possible church, although the details, as at Housesteads, are too insubstantial to form a definitive view.

At South Shields a stone 'table' was found within a minute, square-ended eastern recess set inside the *principia* forecourt in 1878. Insofar as it is possible to attribute a date, the late fourth century (Period 8 or 9) is considered likely, and it has been suggested as a possible church (Bidwell and Speak 1994, 103-4). If so, a context for the presence of Christians at South Shields is the military unit, the *numerus barcariorum Tigrisiensium* thought to have been transferred to South Shields from Mesopotamia (*Arbeia* = the Arabs) in the early fourth century. Clearly, lightermen of Middle-Eastern origin could easily have been Christians, in which case they may be an example of the way in which the faith was transmitted along major trade routes (*ibid*, 45). The tombstone of the Greek, Papias, at Carlisle could be a similar instance.

However, doubts are raised about the South Shields features because the recess, or rather niche, is far too small to have served the same function as an apse. I can find no other parallels in churches for such a small recess in Britain, the trans-Danubian provinces, or in lands such as Jordan and Asia Minor close to the homelands of the *numerus* and where the provision of eastern apses is widely attested (Duval 1994; Hellenkemper 1994; Hoddinott 1963; 1975). An alternative possibility is that the South Shields structure was not a church but a synagogue, in which the niche held a copy of the Torah. Early synagogues, such as that at Priene, occasionally contain small niches or apsidal features on a scale comparable with that at South Shields (Foerster 1981; Hachlili 2001). The 'table', which has been interpreted as a Christian altar, is said to have stood inside the recess and could have held the Ark of the Scrolls and other ritual items. If this was indeed a synagogue and not a church, it represents an example of the way in which an existing building was adapted to a synogogal function. The former *principia* forecourt, now presumably roofed over, could be seen as an assembly hall, whilst adjacent rooms of the *principia* may have continued to operate in a way similar to that hitherto, that is to say for administrative, communal or financial purposes, as was the case elsewhere amongst the Diaspora (White 1990, 60-101).

Most of the archaeological detail for the late Roman town of Corbridge is irrevocably lost, but the plans and displayed remains include two military 'compounds' on the south side of the Stanegate (Bishop and Dore 1988, 1-3). Constructed first under Severus in the early third century and then united into a single unit under Constantius at the turn in the fourth century, the western 'compound' contains a structure variously described as a *schola,* a temple or 'Site 40' (Birley 1954; Lewis 1966, 66-7). It was uncovered in the early stages of investigation by Forster and Knowles before the 1st World War (Forster and Knowles 1913, 243-7), and consists of an east-west oriented nave with a small western apse and one, possibly two, original entrances in the north wall. These were later blocked and a new eastern entrance constructed. The walls had been plastered but the floors were originally earthen and later raised. Outside the eastern entrance, four column bases provide an eastern veranda or porch separating the building from the road.

Neither Site 40 nor any other building in Roman Corbridge has ever been identified as Christian, but that is not to say that a small community of believers was not present. Despite the impressive display and site plan, our knowledge of late Roman Corbridge and its chronological development is very poor. We may surmise that occupation continued into the late fourth and early fifth centuries partly because the coin list extends up to the Theodosian period with occasional issues from the 380s and later, including the important hoard of 48 gold *solidi* deposited about 384 (Archer 1979, 39; Casey 1979, 75).

At some point within the third and fourth centuries the building known as Site 40 was inserted into, and at a slight angle to, the Severan compound wall. Site 40 must, therefore, post-date it. Birley thought that the gate uniting the western with the eastern compounds belonged to a Constantian reconstruction phase, and believed that Site 40 could be placed in the same phase, at the turn of the third and fourth centuries (Birley 1954, 17). However, there is no evidence to say that this is necessarily correct. It could be later, in which case an interpretation as a church in at least one of its phases of use would not be inappropriate. Indeed, given the similarity in the plans of *scholae* (meeting places for guilds and *collegia*) and churches, it could have started as one and ended as the other.

Finally, there is the rectangular 'temple' in the *vicus* north of the fort at Maryport excavated in the 1880s by a local antiquary (Collingwood 1936, 90-3; Lewis 1966, 106; Wilson 1997, 30-1). Aligned on a road, and adjacent to a circular building also thought to be a temple, the building is oriented NE-SW and has a western square-ended projection, an eastern portico and a flagged stone floor. Lewis believed it to be a Mithraeum but the absence of any diagnostic features renders this unlikely. A recent assessment based on extensive geophysical survey maintains the temple interpretation, linking it with the nearby location of many of the Maryport altars, as well as burials and an enclosure wall (Biggins and Taylor 2004, 115). Clearly, not every rectangular building with a square or apsidal projection was necessarily Christian; nevertheless, the presence of burials in an enclosure would be of considerable interest given the absolute rarity in Britain of an association of temples and graves.

Saints

Church dedications and the activities of saints may also provide clues as to the location of churches. Two important early saints, Alban and Martin, both commemorated in dedications, can be eliminated straight away. In the first place the cult of Alban, the earliest British martyr, developed in the later Roman period, but the 'Alban industry' was a High Medieval phenomenon to which the Carlisle example belongs (Jones 1990; Clark 2001). Similarly, in the case of St. Martin, in Gaul there is no evidence that the cult arose much before Prosper took an interest in the mid fifth century, and even then it was probably restricted to Aquitaine until the early sixth century (Stancliffe 1983, 361).

St. Ninian of Whithorn is a slightly different matter, largely because he is referred to by Bede. There has been much debate about Ninian with regard to Bede's references in the *Historia Ecclesiastica*, *Candida Casa* and a lost *Vita* (*HE* III, 4; MacQueen 1961; Thomas 1981; 1992; Clancy 2001). Most scholars now accept that almost all Ninianic dedications belong to the twelfth century, during the reign of David I (MacQueen 1961; Brooke 1987; 1999). The church at Ninekirks, near Brougham, Penrith, with a possible Ninianic element in the place-name remains a conundrum. It lies very close to the Roman cemetery in which possible Christian tombstones are known, and was photographed from the air by St Joseph who thought that crop marks resembled an early monastic site of Irish type (St Joseph 1978, 236-7; pl. 32b). This is, perhaps less likely than an Anglo-Saxon complex which it also resembles.

St. Patrick never attracted cult status in England and Scotland, but his *Letter to Coroticus* and the *Confessio* provide important evidence for Christianity in the late and sub-Roman period. Debate has partly centred on the identification of his home, *Bannavem Taburniae,* so named in the *Confessio.* Several places have been suggested, Dark, for example, favouring a villa near the Bristol Channel (Dark 1993). More convincing, in this writer's opinion, is Charles Thomas's long expressed view (1981; 1992, 16; 1994, 270), that the Hadrian's Wall fort of Birdoswald is a probable *locus*. Birdoswald was known as *Banna* in the *Notitia,* although other places have that name element, but its proximity to the Solway Firth, the Irish Sea and thence Ireland, is, surely, persuasive. Moreover, it is a sequence that mirrors very well some of the latest phases of activity established by recent excavation in the fort itself (Wilmott 1997).

Discussion

As will be apparent from the forgoing discussion, all the archaeological evidence for Christianity in northern Britain during the late Roman period is associated with difficulties. Rather than leave it at that, I have attempted a simple ranking which is set out in Table 2. The least satisfactory category is that of portable objects, because we neither know how those objects came from their place of manufacture to the place of discovery, nor do we know what meaning, if any, was invested in the objects by their owners (Ward Perkins 1978, 639, 651). The latter is crucial, especially as there are so few solely and unambiguously Christian symbols around at the time.

Burials are also contentious. Much of the discussion surrounding Christian burials in Roman Britain is based on the evidence from Poundbury, Dorset, but here Sparey-Green's assertions have been severely criticised. In particular the overall lack of grave goods, the use of gypsum, stone mausolea and the use of stone and lead coffins, and even the orientation and use of family plots, are now seen as conforming to general trends across Britain and are not specifically Christian. Philpott has even questioned whether late Roman Christians in Britain were interested in a specific burial rite, to the extent that the link between burial rite and religious belief at this date maybe less robust than sometimes appears (Philpott 1991, 227). On balance, whilst it can be conceded that some of the known late Roman northern graves *may* be Christian, the amount and quality of the cemetery evidence overall is too small to provide a convincing case one way or the other.

Most of the tombstones and structural remains fall into the category of 'just possible'. The former reflect activities taking place at or very close to their place of discovery, and Handley (2001) has made a case for regarding the formulae attested here as being *possibly* Christian because there are numerous continental examples where that is the case. Clearly, however, there is an element of doubt, as is to be expected in a transitional period during which the church was in the process of defining its identity. If they are Christian, the tombstones indicate a sprinkling of believers from near the central sector of Hadrian's Wall westwards and to the south in the hinterland.

Places of worship represent a different set of problems. Some communities may have used rooms in houses without leaving any trace in the archaeological record of religious practice. What architectural models can be envisaged for those buildings tentatively identified as candidates for churches? At one level is York, the provincial capital, the locus of Constantine the Great's elevation and the centre of the diocese of Eborius, an attendee at the Council of Arles in 314. In order to gain some insight into the form of a church at York, we can instance the possible example at Colchester House, London, and the apsidal building at St. Paul in the Bail, Lincoln (Jones 1994; Sankey 1998), both capable of accommodating relatively large numbers of worshippers, as well as continental examples (Krautheimer 1965). The essential plan of the York cathedral could well have incorporated an east-west basilical layout, perhaps with clerestory, one or more eastern apses, a western narthex and provision for baptism, the whole adorned with images in various forms. Anything less is difficult to imagine in a provincial capital containing the *praeses* and the *dux,* not to mention strong imperial associations.

TABLE 2

Ranked evidence for Christianity in northern Britain

Site	Evidence	Comments
Highly probable or probable		
York	Textual	Bishops at 4th-century Council(s)
York	Roof tile	RIB 2491.160 – *chi-rho* – building material
Maryport	?Tombstone	RIB 856 – *chi-rho*
Vindolanda 2	Stone ?'portable altar'	*Chi-rho* - late 5th/early 6th century
Vindolanda 3	Tombstone	RIB 1722 – *iacit*
Whithorn	Memorial stone	Inscription & *chi-rho*
Just possible		
Carlisle	Tombstone	RIB 955 – formula
Old Carlisle	Tombstone	RIB 908 – quality of epigraphy
Maryport	Tombstone	RIB 862 – quality of epigraphy
Maryport	Tombstone	RIB 863 – quality of epigraphy
Brougham	Tombstone	RIB 786 – formula
Brougham	Tombstone	RIB 787 – formula
Old Penrith	Tombstone	RIB 934 – formula
Catterick	Tombstone	Wright 1967, no. 8 – formula
Cawfields	Tombstone	RIB 1667 – formula
Ireby	Lead tank	Decoration
South Shields	?Synagogue	1878 excavation
Vindolanda 1	?Church	Modern excavation
Housesteads	?Church	1898 excavation
Birdoswald	?Church	Modern excavation
Whithorn	Textual	Bishop Nynia
Possibly Birdoswald	Textual	Family of St. Patrick
Worth considering		
Beadlam, Brough-under-Stainmore, Bywell, Carrawburgh, Chesters, Corbridge, Newcastle, York	Various vessels and trinkets – 'small finds'	See Table 1
Maryport	??Church	1880 excavation
Corbridge	??Church	Pre-1914 excavation in 'compounds'
Ninekirks, Brougham	??Church/monastic	Dedication and aerial photograph
York, Wetherby, Castleford, Hunslet, Glass Houghton, Malton	Burials	Some gypsum and others lacking grave goods

As the provincial capital with a claim to be an imperial city, the northern church in Britain will have been administered from York. However, given the size and geography of northern Britain, and the proliferation of sees in the western Empire during the fourth century, there may have been other bishops, as Thomas has long suggested (1971: 12-19; 1981: 197-201). If so, we have no evidence as to where they were, although Carlisle, Corbridge and Catterick are clear candidates. Alternatively, the idea of a military bishopric comparable with those in Egypt or Syria (Jones 1964, 878) is possible.

With its impressive range of functions, York was a special case within the context of settlement in northern Britain. Other episcopal churches in this remote frontier region may not have been archaeologically recognizable and distinguishable from other buildings. It is worth recalling that elsewhere in the Empire, especially in rural regions much closer to the heart of the Christian world, there are as yet relatively few recognizable church buildings datable to the fourth century (White 1990, 21 et seq). Qirqbize, Syria and Henscir Taglissi in Tripolitania, are known as possible examples that may extend back into the fourth century, but they are conspicuous by their rarity (Tchalenko 1953, I, 332 et seq: II pls. CI-CVII; White op cit.; Ward Perkins and Goodchild 1953, 39-41). So, perhaps the strongest message for Roman Britain is that early church architecture in the fourth century will continue to be elusive, especially as it may owe as much either to the local vernacular building tradition or an association with the military, its clubs and *collegia*, as to the evolutionary stages of basilical designs seen in some major urban churches in other provinces.

With that in mind, buildings interpreted as churches at Vindolanda, Corbridge, Housesteads, Maryport, and Birdoswald are certainly candidates for consideration. Otherwise, whilst no churches have been identified in other northern towns, this lacuna may be partly explained by the fact that only Catterick and Carlisle have seen major investigative programmes in recent years. The best hope so far is at Carlisle, where the alignment of the medieval and later St. Cuthbert's church departs from the standard east-west orientation to a significant degree, but its plan and position fits neatly into a pattern of Roman 'strip' buildings (McCarthy 1982; 1990; 1999). Linkages between Roman buildings – temples, mausolea and domestic structures – with medieval churches, are being increasingly recognised in Britain and more widely in Europe. St. Cuthbert's church is certainly in that category.

The available plans of these putative churches show that they are very small and simple, but this is also the case in other remote parts of frontier or near-frontier regions of the Roman Empire. Some of the small single-naved churches in Macedonia may have been erected as chapels for the garrisons of local forts (Hoddinott 1963: 197-8), and this could also have been the case in parts of Tripolitania, where there are examples connected with the local *gasr* (L. *castrum*) (Ward Perkins and Goodchild 1953, 57-9). Other models can be found in parts of Syria, where they seem to have originated as simple rectangular halls, only changing to basilican form at the end of the fourth century (White 1990, 20 et seq). Comparanda such as these would fit with the scrappy hints of dating currently available for the north British examples. For instance, those at Vindolanda, Housesteads and Birdoswald all seem to be very late fourth if not early fifth century. The possible church, or *schola*/temple, at Corbridge is also relatively late, whilst a late context for the South Shields material would be appropriate if it is reliable in any sense.

This paper did not set out to prove or disprove the presence of fourth-century Christians in northern Britain. The aim was to assess the evidence, which is mostly ambiguous. There is almost nothing that is clear cut, but then we should not expect it. The most persuasive indicators are at Whithorn (Latinus), York (Eborius) and possibly Vindolanda (Brigomaglos), and Maryport (*chi rho*). It does not amount to much, but leaving York to one side, we might just about discern the presence of small communities in the North West. By adding in the slightly less reliable category of 'possible' evidence, we begin to see that those groups of believers may have been replicated across the whole military zone, but in the end Christianity failed to establish itself. Conversion may have taken place in the north, and some of the outward trappings observed, but, with the possible exception of Whithorn, there is little evidence to show that it became embedded in peoples' lives. We know of no influential clerics bullying, persuading and cajoling military or other secular leaders into action, as happened on the continent. Some of the possible churches seem to be so late and small that the congregations could have been formed not by the military, or what was left of them, but by local farmers either building their own church or adapting an existing structure. In the context of economic, administrative and political change around the turn of the fourth and fifth centuries, scattered groups of believers could have had difficulty gaining access to a priest or bishop on a regular basis, whilst the clergy themselves could have been too poorly equipped, educationally and in terms of resources, to have any long-term impact. Against this bleak assessment must be set the idea that very small groups, a Patrician family presence at Birdoswald, someone with sufficient education to commemorate Brigomaglos at Vindolanda, and a small enclave of believers on either side of the Solway at Maryport and Whithorn, kept the flame alight.

References

Archer, S 1979 'Late Roman Gold and Silver Coin Hoards in Britain: A Gazetteer', *in* Casey (ed), 29-65.

Bidwell, P 2006 'Constantius and Constantine at York', *in* Hartley, E, Hawkes, J, Henig, M, & Mee, F (eds) *Constantine the Great, York's Roman* Emperor, 31-40. York Museums and Gallery Trust, York.

Bidwell, P & Speak, S 1994 *Excavations at South Shields Roman Fort. Volume I.* Society of Antiquaries of Newcastle upon Tyne Monograph Series 4.

Biggins, J A & Taylor, D J A 2004 'The Roman fort and vicus at Maryport: geophysical survey 2000-2004', *in* Wilson, R J A & Caruana, I (eds) *Romans on the Solway: Essays in Honour of Richard Bellhouse,* 102-33. Cumberland Westmorland Antiq Archaeol Soc Extra Series 31.

Birley, E 1954 *Corbridge Roman Station (Corstopitum) Northumberland*, Official Guide Book. HMSO, London.

Birley, R, Birley, A, & Blake, J 1999 *The 1998 Excavations at Vindolanda. The Praetorium Site: Interim Report.* Vindolanda Trust, Roman Army Museum, Carvoran.

Bishop, M W & Dore, J N 1988. *Corbridge: Excavations of the Roman Fort and Town 1947-80.* English Heritage, London.

Brooke, D 1987 *The Medieval Cult of Saint Ninian.* Friends of the Whithorn Trust, Whithorn.

Brooke, D 1999 *Saints and Goddesses: The Interface with Celtic Paganism* (The Seventh Whithorn Lecture). Whithorn.

Burnham, B C 2000 'England 3. Hadrian's Wall, Roman Britain in 1999', *Britannia* 31, 385-392.

Casey, P J 1979 'Magnus Maximus in Britain', *in* Casey (ed), 66-79.

Casey, P J (ed) *The End of Roman Britain.* Oxford (=Brit Archaeol Rep, Brit Ser, 71).

Charlesworth, D 1978 'Roman Carlisle', *Archaeological J* 135, 115-37.

CIIC = Macalister, R A S 1945-49. *Corpus Inscriptionem Insularum Celticarum.* The Stationery Office, Dublin.

Clancy, T O 2001 'The Real St. Ninian', *The Innes Review: The Journal of the Scottish Catholic Historical Association* 52, 1-28.

Clark, G 1957 *Archaeology and Society.* Methuen, London.

Clark, J G 2001 'The St. Albans Monks and the Cult of St.Alban: the late Medieval Texts', *in* Henig, M & Lindley, P (eds) *Alban and St. Albans: Roman and Medieval Architecture, Art and Archaeology*, The British Archaeological Association Conference Transactions XXIV, 218-230.

Collingwood, R G 1936 'The Roman fort and settlement at Maryport' *Trans Cumberland Westmorland Antiq Archaeol Soc* NS 2 (36), 85-99.

Cool, H E M 2004 *The Roman Cemetery at Brougham, Cumbria: Excavation 1966-67.* Society for the Promotion of Roman Studies, London (=Britannia Monograph Series 21).

Craig, D 1997 'The Provenance of the Early Christian Inscriptions of Galloway', *in* Hill, P 1997 *Whithorn and St Ninian: The Excavation of a Monastic Town*, 1984-91, 614-20. Sutton/The Whithorn Trust, Stroud.

Crow, J 1995 *Housesteads*. Batsford/English Heritage, London.

Dark, K R 1993 'St. Patrick's *uillula* and the fifth-century occupation of Romano-British villas', *in* Dumville, D N *Saint Patrick AD 493-1993*, 19-24. Boydell Press, Woodbridge.

Duval, N 1994 'L'architecture Chretienne et les practiques liturgiques en Jordanie en rapport avec la Palestine: recherches nouvelle', *in* Painter (ed), 149-212.

Elsner, J 2003 'Archaeologies and agendas: reflections on late ancient Jewish art and early Christian art', *J of Roman Studies* 93, 114-28.

Faull, M L 1977 'British Survival in Anglo-Saxon Northumbria', *in* Laing, L (ed) *Studies in Celtic Survival*, 1-55. Oxford (=Brit Archaeol Rep, Brit Ser 37).

Faull, M & Moorhouse, S (eds) 1981 *West Yorkshire: An Archaeological Survey*. Wakefield.

Ferguson, R S 1893 'On the Roman cemeteries of Luguvallium, and on a sepulchral slab of Roman date found recently', *Trans Cumberland Westmorland Antiq Archaeol Society* OS (12), 365-74.

Fitzpatrick, A P 2004 'The tombstones and inscribed stones' *in* Cool, H E M *The Roman Cemetery at Brougham, Cumbria: Excavation 1966-67*. Society for the Promotion of Roman Studies, London (=Britannia Monograph Series 21).

Foerster, G 1981 'A survey of ancient Diaspora Synagogues,' *in* Levine, L I (ed) *Ancient Synagogues Revealed*, 164-71. Israel Exploration Society.

Forster, R H & Knowles, W C H 1913 'Corstopitum: Report on the Excavations in 1912', *Archaeologia Aeliana* 3rd Ser (10), 230-80.

Forsyth, K 2005 '*Hic memoria perpetua*: the early inscribed stones of southern Scotland in context', *in* Foster, S M & Cross, M (eds), *'Able minds and practised hands': Scotland's Early Medieval Sculpture in the 21st Century*, 113-34. Oxbow, Oxford (=Society for Medieval Archaeology Monograph 23).

Frend, W H C 1992 'Pagans, Christians and 'the Barbarian Conspiracy' of AD 367 in Roman Britain', *Britannia* 23, 121-31.

Frend, W H C 1994 'The Archaeology of the Early Church: An Historical Survey', *in* Painter (ed), 1-16.

Frend, W H C 1996. *The Archaeology of Early Christianity*. Geoffrey Chapman, London.

Frend, W H C 2003 'Roman Britain, a Failed Promise', *in* Carver, M (ed) *The Cross Goes North: Processes of Conversion in Northern Europe AD 300-1300*, 79-91. University of York, York Medieval Press.

Frere, S S 1975 'The Silchester Church: The Excavation by Sir Ian Richmond in 1961', *Archaeologia* 105, 277-302.

Green, C J 1977 'The significance of plaster burials for the recognition of Christian cemeteries', *in* Reece, R (ed), *Burial in the Roman World*, 46-53. CBA Research Rep 22.

Guy, C J 1981 'Roman circular lead tanks in Britain', *Britannia* 12, 271-6.

Hachlili, R 2001 'The archaeology of Judaism', *in* Insoll, T (ed) *Archaeology and World Religion*, 96-122. Routledge, London & New York.

Handley, M A 2001 'The origins of Christian commemoration in late antique Britain', *Early Medieval Europe* 10 (2), 177-9.

Hellenkemper, H 1994 'Early Church Architecture in southern Asia Minor', in Painter (ed), 213-38.

Hill, P 2001 'Whithorn, Latinus and the Origins of Christianity', *in* Hamerow, H & MacGregor, A (eds) *Image and Power in the Archaeology of Early Medieval Britain: essays in honour of Rosemary Cramp*, 23-32. Oxbow Books, Oxford.

Hoddinott, R F 1963 *Early Byzantine Churches in Macedonia and Southern Serbia*. MacMillan, London.

Hoddinott, R F 1975 *Bulgaria in Antiquity: an archaeological introduction*. Ernest Benn, London & Tonbridge.

Hood, A B E (ed & transl) 1978 *St. Patrick: His Writings and Muirchu's Life*. Phillimore, Chichester.

Jones, A H M 1964 *The Later Roman Empire*. Blackwell, Oxford.

Jones, B C 1990 'St Alban's Church and Graveyard, Carlisle', *Trans Cumberland Westmorland Antiq Archaeol Soc* NS 2 (90), 163-181.

Jones, M J 1994 'St Paul in the Bail, Lincoln Britain in Europe?', *in* Painter (ed), 325-47.

King, A 1983 'The Roman Church at Silchester Reconsidered', *Oxford Archaeol J.* 2(2), 225-37.

Krautheimer, R 1965 *Early Christian and Byzantine Architecture*. Penguin, Harmondsworth.

Lewis, M J T 1966 *Temples of Roman Britain*. Cambridge University Press, Cambridge.

MacQueen, J 1961 *St. Nynia: A Study Based on Literary and Linguistic Evidence*. Oliver and Boyd, Edinburgh and London.

Mawer, C F 1995 *Evidence for Christianity in Roman Britain*. Tempus Reparatvm, Oxford (=Brit Archaeol Rep, Brit Ser 243).

McCarthy, M R 1982 'Thomas, Chadwick and post-Roman Carlisle', *in* Pearce, S (ed) *The Early Church in Western Britain and Ireland: Studies Presented to C A Ralegh Radford*, 241-56. Oxford (=Brit Archaeol Rep, Brit Ser 102).

McCarthy, M R 1990 *A Roman, Anglian and Medieval Site at Blackfriars Street, Carlisle: Excavations 1977-9*. Cumberland Westmorland Antiq Archaeol Soc Research Series 4, Kendal.

McCarthy, M R 1999 'Carlisle and St Cuthbert', *Durham Archaeol J* 14-15, 59-67.

Ottaway, P 1993 *Roman York*. English Heritage/Batsford, London.

Painter, K 1994 'Introduction', *in* Painter (ed), xv-xxvii.

Painter, K (ed) 1994 *'Churches Built in Ancient Times' Recent studies in Early Christian Archaeology*. London (=Society Antiquaries of London Occasional Paper 16).

Petts, D 2003 *Christianity in Roman Britain*. Tempus, Stroud.

Philpott, R 1991 *Burial Practices in Roman Britain: a survey of grave treatment and furnishing AD 43-410*. Oxford (=Brit Archaeol Rep, Brit Ser 219).

Radford, C A R 1971 'Christian Origins in Britain', *Medieval Archaeology* 15, 1-12.

Ramm, H G 1971 'The End of Roman York', *in* Butler, R M (ed) *Soldier and Civilian in Roman Yorkshire,* 179-99. Leicester University Press, Leicester.

RCHM 1962 *Volume I Eburacum Roman York*. Royal Commission on Historical Monuments, England. HMSO.

RIB = Collingwood, R G & Wright, R P 1965 *The Roman Inscriptions of Britain*. Oxford University Press, Oxford.

Richmond, I A 1945 'A Roman vat of lead, from Ireby, Cumberland', *Trans Cumberland Westmorland Antiq Archaeol Soc* 45, NS, 163-71.

Sankey, D 1998 'Cathedrals, granaries and urban vitality in late Roman London', *in* Watson, B (ed) *Roman London: recent archaeological work including papers given at a seminar held in the Museum of London on 16th November 1996*, 78-82. (=Journal Roman Archaeology Supplement 24). Rhode Island, Portsmouth.

Sherley-Price, L (transl) 1955 Bede *A History of the English Church and People*. Penguin, Harmondsworth.

Shotter, D 2000 *Roman Coins from North-West England: Second Supplement*. Centre for North-West Regional Studies, Lancaster.

Sparey-Green, C 2003 'Late Roman Cemeteries in Britain', in Carver, M (ed) *The Cross Goes North: Processes of Conversion in Northern Europe AD 300-1300*, 93-107. University of York, York Medieval Press.

St. Joseph, J K 1978 'Aerial reconnaissance: recent results, 46', *Antiquity* 52, 236-8.

Stancliffe, C 1983 *St. Martin and his Hagiographer*. Clarendon Press, Oxford.

Swift, C 1997 *Ogam Stones and the Earliest Irish Christians*, Maynooth Monographs Series Minor II. Maynooth.

Tchalenko, G 1953-1958. *Villages Antiques de la Syria du Nord*. Paris.

Thomas, C 1971 *The Early Christian Archaeology of North Britain*. Oxford University Press, Oxford.

Thomas, C 1981 *Christianity in Roman Britain to AD 500*. Batsford, London.

Thomas, C 1992 *Whithorn's Christian Beginnings* (The First Whithorn Lecture). Friends of the Whithorn Trust, Whithorn.

Thomas, C 1994 'The Eastern Mediterranean and the Western Provinces: A British Perspective', in Painter (ed), 269-78.

Thomas, C 1998 *Christian Celts: Messages and Images*. Tempus, Stroud.

Toynbee, J M C 1953 'Christianity in Roman Britain', *J British Archaeological Association* 3rd Ser 16, 1-24.

Toynbee, J M C 1963 *Art in Roman Britain*. 2nd edn, Phaidon, London.

Ward-Perkins, J B 1978 'The role of craftsmanship in the formation of early Christian art', *Atti del IX Congresso Internazionale di Archaeologia Cristiana*, Volume I, 637-52. Roma.

Ward-Perkins, J B & Goodchild, R G 1953 'The Christian Antiquities of Tripolitania', *Archaeologia* 95, 1-84.

Watts, D 1988 'Circular lead tanks and their significance for Romano-British Christianity', *Antiquaries J* 68 Pt II, 210-222.

Watts, D 1991 *Christians and Pagans in Roman Britain*. Routledge, London & New York.

Watts, D 1998 *Religion in Late Roman Britain: forces of change*. Routledge, London & New York.

White, L M 1990 *The Social Origins of Christian Architecture*. Harvard Theological Studies, Valley Forge, Pennsylvania. Trinity Press International.

Wilmott, T 1997 *Birdoswald: Excavations of a Roman Fort on Hadrian's Wall and its Successor Settlement 1987-92*. London (=English Heritage Archaeological Report 14).

Wilmott, T 2004 'Roman Brougham in its Regional Setting', *in* Cool (ed), 2-8.

Wilson, R J A 1997 'Maryport from the first to the fourth centuries', *in* Wilson, R J A (ed) *Roman Maryport and its Setting: essays in Memory of Michael G. Jarrett*, 17-39. Trustees of the Senhouse Roman Museum, Maryport.

Wood, I 2004 'The Final Phase', *in* Todd, M (ed) *A Companion to Roman Britain*, 428-42. Blackwell, Oxford.

Wright, R P 1967 'Roman Britain in 1966. II Inscriptions', *J Roman Studies* 57, 204-10.

6. Britain and the Continent in the Fifth and Sixth Centuries: the evidence of Ninian

Ian Wood

A chronological problem

Eighth-century texts link Ninian to the continent, first by claiming that he travelled to Rome, where he received instruction, and secondly, through the dedication to St Martin of the church at Whithorn. According to later medieval tradition he was active in the early part of the fifth century (*Bede*, ed Plummer 1896, 128-9): the Martinian dedication would thus belong in the earliest phase of the development of the cult of the bishop of Tours, and the Rome journey could be seen in the context of the last years of the empire. This dating, however, has long been a matter of debate,[1] and the problem of Ninian's chronology has been thrown into particularly sharp focus by Thomas Clancy's argument (2001) that he is to be identified with Finnian,[2] an Irish monastic figure, possibly of British extraction (Sharpe 1984; Dumville 1984),[3] who corresponded with Gildas (Columbanus ep. 1, 6-7), and was the author of a penitential (Bieler (ed) 1975, 74-95). If correct, Ninian was active in the sixth, rather than the fifth century – although how early or late would be a matter for debate, along with the problematic chronology of Gildas himself.[4] Placed in the later period, the Martinian dedication of Whithorn could be set alongside the substantial development of the saint's cult, following Perpetuus' rebuilding of the basilica of Tours in the late fifth century (Gregory of Tours, *Decem Libri Historiarum*, X, 31), though one should note that, with the possible exception of Winnoc, who is usually thought to have come from Armorica (*ibid*, V, 21),[5] Britons do not appear in Gregory of Tours' voluminous writings on Martin. Winnoc, however, is an exception worthy of note: he is described as a *Brito* coming *de Britanniis*, which could refer to the old Roman provinces of Britain. Moreover, he was *en route* for Jerusalem, when, in c577, he stopped in Tours, where he was persuaded to become a priest. In addition, Gregory's friend and contemporary, Venantius Fortunatus, in his verse *Life* of the saint, refers to winter as the time when the Ocean prevents the Britons from having access to commerce – implying regular summer trade, if not pilgrimage (Venantius Fortunatus, *Vita Martini*, III 26). Yet while it might be easy to find a sixth-century context for the Martinian dedication at Whithorn, it would be harder to find a parallel for Ninian's training in Rome in the same period.

In fact both the journey to Rome and the dedication to Martin are problematic. It is not clear that Ninian himself was responsible for the dedication of his church to the saintly bishop of Tours – that could have come later, though it is unlikely to have been introduced by the Northumbrians, when one considers the near-absence of Martin in the works of Bede, despite a reference to his

---

[1] The material up until 1997 is usefully gathered in Hill 1997, 1-4.
[2] For some reservations, see Barrow 2004.
[3] For an overview of the debate, see Charles-Edwards 2000, 291.
[4] For a brief resumé of the discussions, together with an argument for a late date, Stancliffe 1997, 177-81.
[5] I am indebted to Alex Woolf for reminding me of the importance of Winnoc.

floruit in the *Chronica Minora* (Bede, *De* Temporibus, 22),[6] and his being one of the few names to be retained in Jones' reconstruction of the *Kalendarium* (*Bede*, ed Jones 1975a, 577). The dedication might, however, reflect Frankish influence during the seventh century (for Anglo-Saxon parallels, see Blair 2005, 220). Contact between Galloway and Francia in that period can be identified archaeologically, for instance in the E-ware found both at Tours and Whithorn (Wooding 1996, 76-7) – suggesting a continuation of the trade noted by Venantius Fortunatus.

On the other hand, Ninian's supposed visit to Rome could reflect Anglo-Saxon concerns rather than any historical journey. Leaving aside (at least for the time being) the possibility that he is to be identified with the Finnian or Findbarr of the Irish sources, our early evidence for Ninian is essentially Northumbrian, being made up of Bede's comments in the *Historia Ecclesiastica* (III 4) and the poem in the *Miracula Nyniae* from the circle of Alcuin (*Miracula Nynie Episcopi*).[7] Since Bede had little respect for British clergy (see *Historia Ecclesiastica* I 22), Ninian presented him with a problem: here was a figure whose saintly reputation was too strong to ignore. Moreover he had indulged in the one activity which Bede decried the Britons for avoiding: he had evangelised pagans – admittedly the southern Picts rather than the English, and he did so, supposedly long before Columba's work further north (*ibid*, III 4: compare I 22). In emphasising Ninian's training in Rome, Bede and the poet of the *Miracula Nyniae* obliterate the saint's British origins, making him instead an honorary Roman (Wood 2003, 125-7; Orton *et al* 2007, 128-9). Presumably there was an earlier tradition linking Ninian with Rome, but the story we have seems to reflect an Anglo-Saxon retelling of the tale. In other words, we are faced with a saint who may have existed in the fifth or the sixth century, and whose supposed connections with the continent may tell us more about seventh- and eighth-century interests than about his own sphere of action.

Yet it is perhaps best not to be too sceptical: Bede had some reason for linking Ninian with Rome – and the Petrus stone suggests that there had been some contact between Whithorn and Rome by the start of the seventh century (Forsyth 2005, 127-30). When we try to understand the possible links, however, we should remember that connections between Galloway and the continent in the early fifth century were very different from those in the mid-sixth. What I shall do in the second half of this paper is to set out two separate sketches, one for each century. Although I shall make some reference to archaeology and to the inscribed stones of the western seaboard of Britain, I shall concentrate largely on written texts, on the assumption that they will tell us most about the general ecclesiastical context of Ninian's world. Of course, the sketches will oversimplify – and they will not be as chronologically precise as one would like. First, however, I shall look briefly at the difference between British contacts with the continent in the fifth and those in the sixth centuries.

Changing contacts between Britain and the continent

Scholars have sometimes lumped the evidence for contact between Britain and the continent from the fifth century together with that from the sixth (Knight 1996, 113-4). This is to combine information from two very different periods – as indeed, some archaeologists have noted.[8] In fact, we have good written information for contacts up to the 460s, and renewed evidence for an apparently changed world after the opening decades of the sixth century: in between the picture is less clear. This may be a meaningless lacuna in our sources – and certainly communication did not stop altogether.[9] On the other hand, disruption in Gaul was significant at precisely this time (Wood 1984; 1987; 1992). It included migration from Britain to Brittany – though the

---

[6] In addition to the dedication of Ninian's church, there are references to Martin in Bede's *Historia Ecclesiastica* (I 26, II 5, III 4, IV 18) in the context of Augustine at Canterbury and the burial of John the Archanter at Tours. There appears to have been no reference in the *Chronicon Maior*, though Martin's name is added in some manuscripts.

[7] Recent discussions have been Lapidge 1996, 386-90: Orchard 2000, 27-34.

[8] Wooding 1996, 78, in talking of the economy, does not see the sixth century as continuing the patterns of the fifth and earlier.

[9] This depends considerably on when one dates Patrick's *Confessio* and Gildas' *De Excidio Britonum*.

chronology and the scale of the migration is open to question (Galliou and Jones 1991). And of course, the migration itself may have strengthened some lines of communication between Britain and the continent. Migrants who left Britain early in the fifth century, such as Faustus of Riez, were in continuing contact with Britain even after their departure (Sidonius Apollinaris, ep. IX, 9). It is possible that Mansuetus, a British bishop present at the Council of Tours in 461, still had links with his insular home (Council of Tours 461, ed Munier 1963). If so, he might have provided information on the developing cult of Martin – which would be of some importance for our understanding of the cult at Whithorn. Riothamus, the curious military leader who appears in Gaul at the head of a substantial army, intent on supporting the (already failed) emperor Anthemius, may not have lost contact with Britain after settling in the region of Lyons around the year 470 (Jordanes *Getica* XLV, 238; Sidonius Apollinaris, ep. III, 9; Wood 2004, 438).

The following decades, however, saw the expansion of Frankish power over most of northern Gaul, and while the Franks can be seen as agents and heirs of the Roman Empire, that expansion was largely achieved by fighting. Already Childeric had been involved in campaigns in the Loire valley (Gregory, *Decem Libri Historiarum* II 18-19). At some point before his death in 481 Genovefa secured the survival of captives taken by the Frankish king (*Vita Genovefae* VI 25)*. Her *Vita* also records that the city of Paris was beseiged by the Franks for ten years (*ibid* VIII, 34), which may be an exaggeration, but given that the text was probably written in the 520s (Heinzelmann and Poulin 1986, 178), the story is likely to have had a kernel of truth. The last years of the fifth century must also have been the period in which a small Frankish kingdom was set up in Le Mans, soon to be taken over by Clovis (Gregory, *Decem Libri Historiarum* II 42). Procopius, writing in Byzantium, supplies some garbled information about considerable resistance put up against the Franks by the *Arborychi*, who are plausibly seen as the people of Armorica (Procopius *Wars*, V xii, 14). Since he says that the two peoples were able to come to terms because they were both catholic, the conflict would seem to have continued until after the baptism of Clovis, which can be best dated to 508 (Shanzer 1998).

At the same time, the migration of the Angles and Saxons gained pace, both leading to settlement in Britain and disrupting the eastern seaways. By the mid-sixth century, Procopius seems to have understood the British West as constituting a different island from the Saxon East (Procopius *Wars*, VIII xx, 4-6; Thompson 1980a). Thus, while disruption in northern Gaul need not have severed links between Galloway, Gaul and Rome altogether, it is unlikely that communication between Britain and the continent was as easy between 470 and 520 as it had been in 400; declining stability in Gaul, and the arrival of the Saxons in southern Britain must have had an effect. And while links between Britain and Gaul may have become easier towards the mid-sixth century, the route to Rome would have become less safe with the outbreak of war between the Ostrogoths and Byzantines in the 530s. The context in which an early-fifth-century Ninian developed contacts with Gaul and Rome would be very different from that in which a mid-sixth-century one operated.

A fifth-century context for Ninian?

If we opt for the early fifth century as Ninian's *floruit*, we are dealing with the last years of Roman Britain, with the withdrawal of troops (though probably not the *limitanei* of the Wall),[10] and of the upper echelons of the administration: equally important in the south, perhaps, was the severing of links with the centre of the Empire which had allowed absentee senatorial landlords to exploit the villas that we know they held (Gerontios, *Vita Melaniae*, 11). At the same time it is clear that there was initial survival of some aspects of Roman administration, which gradually lost out to warlords who presented themselves as kings. We hear about this survival largely from ecclesiastical sources, for instance from comments on the activities of tribunes in the *Life*

---

[10] For an argument in favour of continuity on the Wall, see Orton, Wood and Lees 2007, 110-5.

of Germanus of Auxerre by Constantius of Lyons (Constantius *Vita Germani,* 15),[11] and from Gildas's comments on the council, which under the leadership of the *superbus tyrannus* invited in the Saxons (Gildas *De Excidio Britonum* 23, 1). In the *De Excidio*, this image of surviving Roman provincial government is followed by the picture of the kings of Gildas' own day. These same sources are, of course, crucial for our understanding of the early-fifth-century church in Britain. To them one may add the related evidence for the mission of Palladius to Ireland, and, albeit difficult to date, the *Confessio* and *Epistola* of Patrick.

Constantius presents us with an essentially sub-Roman picture. Germanus comes to Britain because of the growth of Pelagian heresy in the island – a growth which itself was probably caused by the success of the imperial authorities in persecuting the sect elsewhere in the empire, rather than there being any indigenous Pelagian traditions – despite the fact that Pelagius himself came from Britain (Wood 1984, 6-9). The exact circumstances of Germanus' mission are unclear, not least because of a conflict within our sources. In the *Vita Germani* Britons appeal to the Gallic bishops for help against the spread of Pelagianism, and a council responds by sending Germanus and Lupus of Troyes (Constantius *Vita Germani,* 12). According to Prosper of Aquitaine, it was Palladius, presumably a Roman deacon of that name, who persuaded pope Celestine (422-32) to send Germanus to Britain (Prosper *Chronicon*, s. a. 429). The pope sent the same Palladius to the Irish believers in Christ two years later (Prosper *Chronicon*, s. a. 431; see the discussion in Hanson 1968, 52-4). Exactly who instigated the visit of Germanus is thus unclear: both the pope and a Gallic synod could have been involved. Either way, Germanus set out for Britain, accompanied by Lupus of Troyes. He arranged a public disputation, which he won (Constantius *Vita Germani,*14). He then went on to visit the shrine of St Alban (*ibid,* 16). This episode is more fully recorded in what seems to be the earliest *Passio* of the martyr, the Ur-version of which was apparently written in Auxerre on Germanus' instructions. In this account the bishop of Auxerre opened the tomb, inserted some relics of other saints which he had brought with him, and took away earth stained with the martyr's blood.[12] In Constantius' account, before returning to Gaul Germanus helped deal with a Saxon attack, culminating in the so-called Alleluia victory, when the invaders fled at the sound of the Christian cry (Constantius *Vita Germani,* 17-18). Once Germanus had returned to Gaul, however, the Pelagian problem erupted again. According to Constantius, the bishop of Auxerre made a second visit to Britain, this time accompanied by Severus of Trier (Constantius *Vita Germani,* 25). Some have seen the second visit as a mere doublet of the first, though this is unnecessary (eg Chadwick 1955, 255-6). Moreover, according to Constantius, it was as a result of this second visit that the Pelagians were not merely defeated, but actually condemned to exile (Wood 1984, 17) Peter Hill (2001) has made the intriguing suggestion that it might have been a group of Pelagian exiles who established the first Christian community in Whithorn. This, if correct, of course tells us only about the earliest Christians in the Machars, and may say nothing about Ninian himself – he was presumably not a Pelagian, although he may have had to deal with a heretical community. Germanus' visits may, thus, have had an indirect significance for Whithorn and Ninian, but the bishop of Auxerre's own actions seem to have been confined to the south, even, perhaps, to the south-east, of Britain. The tradition that the Alleluia victory took place at Llanarmon-yn-Yal, in North Wales, is no longer accepted, leaving the most likely site for the battle somewhere in south-east England, while the religious incidents would seem to belong to the London region and Verulamium.

The *Life of Germanus* does, however, illustrate a period of papal interest in Britain, and thus could provide a general context for Ninian's Roman journey. Whether the inspiration for the bishop of Auxerre's visit came from the pope, or whether, alternatively, Germanus simply sought papal approval for his first visit to Britain, the information he brought back is likely to have been crucial in prompting pope Celestine to send a mission under Palladius to the believers already present in Ireland (Charles-Edwards 1993) – suggesting an interesting line of

---

[11] For the meaning of the term in this context, see Wood 1984, 10, n 81.
[12] Unfortunately the earliest version of the *Passio* is still unedited, though later recensions were edited by Meyer 1904, 60-1. For the date, see Sharpe 2001, 30-7.

communication between that island and its neighbour to the east. It is not clear how long-lasting was the impact of Palladius' work in Ireland, and whether some achievements later ascribed to Patrick should be acknowledged as reflecting the activities of the earlier Roman envoy (Dumville 1993, 59-88 gathers the evidence). Nevertheless, Palladius provides a glimpse of a momentary opening up of connections between Rome, Britain and southern Ireland, and hence perhaps of the world of the Irish Sea more generally. And there may be some further reflection of those connections in some of the hagiography, admittedly composed rather later: for instance the *Life of Ailbhe*, in which the saint studies with pope Hilary (461-8) (*Vita s. Albei*, 4-18). This might be a context for Ninian's return from Rome and his evangelisation of the Southern Picts. At the very moment that imperial authority was in decline, papal interest in Britain and Ireland was developing – though not for long: the arrival in Italy first of the Huns and then of the Goths led to a diminution of papal horizons in the West[13] which would not be fully restored until the days of Gregory the Great (590-604).[14]

Connections between Ireland and the continent, though not stretching as far as Rome, are apparent in both Patrick's *Confessio* and his *Letter to Coroticus*. In the former text he talks of his longing to return to Britain to see his family, and even to go on to visit the brethren in Gaul and (more obscurely) to see the face of the saints of the Lord (Patrick *Confessio*, 43). In the *Epistola* he mentions a custom of the Gallo-Roman Christians, who, he says, send holy men to the Franks and other barbarians to ransom their captives (Patrick *Epistola ad Coroticum*, 14). This suggests some knowledge of the Gallo-Roman Church – perhaps even specific knowledge of a figure like Genovefa, who, as we have already seen, secured the safety of some captives held by the Franks (*Vita Genovefae* VI, 25).[15] Unfortunately, it has proved impossible to add any precision on the matter of Patrick's continental contacts. His famous trek across a deserted landscape, having escaped by sea from Ireland, is as likely to have taken place in Britain as in Brittany (Thompson 1985, 22-34) – and Patrick's own account seems to have been influenced by the Biblical story of Christ's wandering in the wilderness. Those accounts that do give us precise information about time spent by Patrick on the continent were unfortunately written in the seventh century and later (Charles-Edwards 2000, 183-4). If they do contain any early tradition, it is important to note that they link Patrick with Auxerre, apparently in the time of Amator, Germanus' predecessor as bishop (Muirchú, *Vita Patricii*, I 6-9),[16] and not with Tours: they, therefore, offer no help in understanding the cult of Martin at Whithorn.

Patrick thus gives us only slight hints of contacts between Ireland and the continent, though not necessarily directly with Rome or with Tours. On the other hand his own origins might bring us closer to Whithorn – if *Bannavem Taberniae* (or whatever place name is hidden under that jumble of letters) can be equated with the fort of *Banna*, or Birdoswald, on Hadrian's Wall.[17] There are those who would place Patrick's origins in Wales or on the Severn, and hitherto there has been no way of deciding finally between the various different hypotheses (Hanson 1968, 113-6; Thompson 1985, 9-13). Similar problems arise when one turns to Patrick's *Letter to Coroticus*, who has proved equally elusive. The recipient might belong in Strathclyde, in Wales, or even, following Edward Thompson, in Ireland (Thompson 1980b).

The chronology of Patrick's career is, of course, a matter of considerable disagreement. There are those who place his death in the 460s and others in the 490s (Dumville 1993, 29-33). The later date would suggest continuing links with the continent, though not necessarily with Tours or Rome, into the last decades of the fifth century. What Patrick has to say about his own childhood, which might be dated to the first or the second quarter of the fifth century, suggests that we are dealing with what is still a Roman society, not dissimilar to that portrayed by Constantius in the *Vita Germani*. In other words, if we date Ninian to the fifth century, he was,

---

[13] For a dimunition after the arrival of the Goths, see Shanzer and Wood 2002, 125-6.

[14] For papal contacts with Francia in the intervening period, see Wood 2006, 223-42.

[15] For the ransom of captives in the south of Gaul, see Shanzer and Wood 2002, 350-6.

[16] On the current rejection of the accuracy of this tradition, van Egmond 2006, 33, with 81 on the *Vita Amatoris* and its possible influence on Muirchú.

[17] A link between Patrick and Birdoswald is denied by Wilmott 1997, 231. See also MacCarthy, this volume.

like Patrick, a member of a late- or immediately post-Roman world. In trying to understand his supposed connections with Rome, one might turn to the evidence of papal involvement in the two missions of Germanus to Britain, and perhaps more suggestively, in the sending of Palladius to Ireland – which, as we have seen, might have inspired Ninian's own missionary work among the southern Picts. Whether the introduction of the cult of Martin is likely in this context is another matter. Despite the significance of Sulpicius Severus' *Vita Martini*, it is not clear that the confessor's cult really took off at Tours until the episcopate of Perpetuus in the 460s (Van Dam 1993, 18-20), by which time, as we have seen, the Loire valley was certainly becoming a rather unsettled region.

A sixth-century context for Ninian?

If we decide to place Ninian in the context of contacts between Britain and the continent in the mid-sixth century, the picture is different, even if we ignore the developments in the south and east, where some level of Anglo-Saxon migration was leading to political reorganisation, and the formation of the kingdoms of Sussex, Kent, Essex, Wessex and East Anglia.[18] For the West our most important source is Gildas, even though, like Patrick, he is hard to pin down chronologically, with *floruits* given for any time in the period from 490 to 570.[19] Whatever his dates, the picture he gives of his own time is not that of the Roman world of Germanus, into which Patrick was born. Gildas looks back to that time, but presents it as at least three generations earlier.[20] Even so, his education seems still to have been remarkably classical (Lapidge 1984; Herren 1990). Again, like Patrick and Coroticus, he is hard to place geographically: he probably belongs in the western part of Britain, though arguably beyond the reach of the five kings he lampoons: Constantine of Dumnonia, Vortipor of Demetia, Maglocunus of Gwynedd, and the less certainly placed Aurelius Caninus and Cuneglasus. The earlier of the two saint's *Lives* devoted to him claims that he was born in Strathclyde and ended his life in Brittany, at St Gildas de Rhuys, having made one major journey to Rome and Ravenna (*Vita Gildae auctore monacho Ruiensi*, 1, 13-14, 28-30). This gives us a geographical range strikingly similiar to that in which Ninian is said to have operated. Unfortunately the *Life* was written in the eleventh century, and there is no reason to believe its detail. If Gildas did indeed die at Rhuys, which is plausible, he must, at some late stage in his life, have joined those migrants from Britain to whom he alludes in the *De Excidio* (Gildas, 25, 1). On the other hand, he says nothing specific of contacts between Britain and the continent when talking about his own day. He does, however, show some knowledge of Gallic writing of the fourth and fifth centuries, not least the works of Sulpicius Severus (Kerlouegan 1987, 85-6; Wright 1984, 110-1, 114).

Gildas' move to the continent is only recorded in later traditions, like that of a number of Breton saints of British origin. The only *Life* relating to this group of migrant saints that has some claim to belonging to the seventh or (at the latest) eighth century is that of Samson (ed Flobert 1997). This is a remarkable, and difficult, text: difficult because it is written in somewhat ungrammatical Latin, which is often obscure (to say the least), because its tone is hard to establish (the author seems to have had an extraordinary sense of humour, and it is not clear whether this vitiates its value as a source), and because it seems to make claims which are scarcely credible (Wood 1988, 380-4). For all that, it remains the most extensive pre-Carolingian source to provide information on contacts between Britain and the continent in the post-Roman period – not just in its account of Samson's life, but also in the author's (somewhat confusingly dated) account of his own journey to Britain and Ireland to research the biography of his subject (*Vita Samsonis*, Prologus).

---

[18] The best gathering of material is Bassett 1989.

[19] A brief survey of the literature, together with an argument in favour of a late date is given by Stancliffe 1997, 177-81.

[20] He talks of the grandchildren of Ambrosius Aurelianus being active in his own day; Gildas, *De Excidio Britonum* 25, 3.

According to the *Life* Samson was the son of a Demetian father and a mother from Gwent, both of them aristocratic (*Vita Samsonis* I, 1). He was given to the Church as a child, and sent to Illtud (*ibid* I, 9), who, according to tradition, was based at Llantwit Major. After his ordination as deacon by bishop Dubricius (*ibid* I, 13), Samson left Illtud's monastery and went to the community of Pirus (*ibid* I, 20), probably that on Caldey. He then briefly returned home, where he supervised the entry of his close relatives into the monastic life ((*ibid* I, 29). When Pirus died (having fallen down a well while inebriated), Samson gained Dubricius' permission to accompany a group of Irish, returning from a journey to Rome, to their homeland (*ibid* I, 36-7). Having subsequently returned to Britain, he became a hermit on the banks of the Severn (*ibid* I, 40), but was made abbot of a community established (supposedly) by Germanus (*ibid* I, 42). Thereafter, he was elevated to the episcopate (*ibid* I, 44), but determined to depart for the continent (*ibid* I, 45). Having made a brief stop in Wales, he crossed Cornwall, evangelising and performing miracles (*ibid* I, 48-51), and sailed for mainland Europe. He established a monastery at Dol (*ibid* I, 52), but then became involved in Franco-Breton politics, intervening with the Merovingian king Childebert on behalf of Judwal, whose freedom he secured (*ibid* 1, 53-9), before returning to Dol to die (*ibid* I, 61).

Charles Thomas noted the importance of this text for any understanding of British Christianity (Thomas 1994, 223-36). For our present purposes, however, it is more important in illustrating contacts between Ireland, Wales, Cornwall, Brittany and Francia. Moreover, for Samson we do have one very specific date, since he attended the third Council of Paris held at some point between 556 and 573 (Council of Paris 556-73 (ed Gaudemet & Basdevant 1989) – in other words he was active in Francia a full generation before the move of the Irishman Columbanus to the continent (for the date of Columbanus' move, see Wood 1998, 105-6), and a little before the arrival of Winnoc in Tours. His presence at the council perhaps strengthens the likelihood that he was indeed a figure of some importance in Frankish politics. And this might further be supported by the fact that a Merovingian prince, who died in 578, was given the extremely rare name Samson (Gregory of Tours *Decem Libri Historiarum* V, 22).[21]

More than the evidence of Gildas, the *Life of Samson*, thus, provides a number of analogies for what Bede tells us of Ninian. We meet a group of Irishmen returning from Rome: according to the author they were very learned (*peritissimi*) and they were philosophers (*Vita Samsonis*, I, 37). Of course, these are Irishmen, rather than Britons, and there is plenty of evidence of Irish visits to Rome in the seventh century and later, not least in the context of the Easter controversy.[22] But the events of Samson's career belong several generations earlier. As we shall see, there may be some additional Irish evidence for this period that is worth bringing into the picture. Further, although Samson takes us no closer to Tours than did Germanus, or any of the fifth-century figures apart from Mansuetus we have investigated, he does take us to Paris, and thus to the world of Neustria. Further, Samson does not take us into north Britain, but in terms of his own career only to the south coast of Wales and (presumably) southern Ireland. He, therefore, does not take us even as far north as the famous Penmachno stone, with its funerary inscription for Avitor and its possible date of the consulship of Justin in 540 – though this is open to question (Knight 1996, 115-6; Handley 2001, 192-4). If the inscription does indeed boast a consular date, then 'a British cleric who had visited Lyon, which lay on the main route to Rome', provides another possible Briton to go alongside Ninian. And Samson's activity in Britain probably overlapped with the date of the Penmachno stone, of 540 or later.

The *Life of Samson*, then, gives us a possible parallel for some aspects of Ninian's career if we choose to place him in the mid-sixth century. At first sight, this is more useful than anything to be found in the *De Excidio* of Gildas. The latter could, however, help provide a context for Ninian, if we follow Clancy and accept the identification of Ninian with Finnian or Uinniau, since Columbanus mentions correspondence between Gildas and Finnian in a letter written to pope Gregory the Great in c600 (Columbanus, ep. I, 6-7; Sharpe 1984; Dumville 1984). If

---

[21] For the rarity of the name, see *Vita Samsonis,* ed Flobert 1997, 11.
[22] Charles-Edwards 2000, 411, sees Columbanus as essentially beginning the tradition of Irish appeals to Rome.

Ninian and Finnian really were one and the same person a number of points follow from this reference – as well as from what else can be deduced of the history of Finnian (Clancy 2001).[23] Unfortunately the letter itself does not survive, though a section of it has been plausibly identified with the fourth of the Gildas *Fragmenta* (ed and transl Winterbottom 1978, 81, 144). The passage deals with monks moving from one monastery to another, approving the move if the abbot of the first house is truly degenerate, but urging caution if the monk is only looking for a community that he thinks is of a higher standard to that in which he is resident. The situations envisaged are remarkably close to those depicted in the *Life of Samson*. More important in the present context, assuming this to be a fragment of the letter to Finnian, we here see Gildas responding to a question about monastic discipline. The implication would seem to be that Gildas was perceived as an authority by Finnian, and was thus, presumably, older. Gildas' monastic authority is also apparent from his Penitential (ed Bieler 1975, 60-5), which has been seen as lying at the start of the penitential tradition (Sharpe 1984, 191-205). That of Finnian is presumably very slightly more recent in date. Equally important, both men belonged to an earlier generation than that of Columbanus, who indeed looked up to them, and introduced their tradition of penitential writing to the continent (Charles-Edwards 1997).

There is some Irish hagiographical evidence for contact between Ireland and the continent in the generations before Columbanus, though unfortunately the dating of most Irish saint's *Lives* is uncertain, and few of them can be placed as early as the eighth century. Among those saints whose *floruit* would seem to be mid-sixth century, there is Mochta, who was supposedly sent to Rome by an angel to collect scriptures (*Vita s. Mochtei*, 2). More interesting, according to his *vita*, Tigernach went to Rome to collect relics, and travelled via St Martin's at Tours (*Vita s. Tigernachi*, 5-6). The *Life of Columba of Terryglas* claimed that the saint collected relics from Rome, returning via the shrine of Martin (*Vita s. Columbae de Tir dá Glas*). Perhaps particularly significant, his master was Finnian of Clonard, who supposedly blessed his journey. As for Finnian himself – one of the figures who has been identified with Ninian – his *vita* explicitly says that he did not go to Rome, being forbidden to do so by an angel (*Vita s. Finniani*, 9). This presents a clear conflict with the Northumbrian accounts of Ninian, but it raises the possibility that, despite Anglo-Saxon tradition, it was not Ninian himself who went to Rome and who returned with relics of Martin, but one of his pupils. None of the Irish texts listed here, however, is clearly early in date, and they may all present a reconstuction of what later generations thought connections between the Irish world, Rome and the continent ought to have been in the mid-sixth century.

Columbanus provides a useful chronological terminus to this discussion. He is usually seen as the first great Irish ascetic to head for the continent, where he undoubtedly had a major impact (most recently assessed in Charles-Edwards 2000, 344-90). He also knew both Tours (Jonas, *Vita Columbani* I, 22) and the writings of Sulpicius Severus (Wright 1997, 76-8). While he never actually made it to Rome, he expressed a desire to visit the city of Peter, and he revered the papacy, even though he was critical of its stance over Easter and over the Tricapitoline schism (Columbanus, ep. I, 8 (pp10-11), V, 11, 15-16 (pp 48-51, 53-55). If we accept any of the accounts of pilgrimages made to Rome by Ninian, Mochta, Tigernach or Columba of Tallaght, this has implications for how we should understand Columbanus' decision to head for the continent – the notion of *peregrinatio* on its own is not quite enough, for *peregrinatio* might only take one as far as the Scottish Isles, as in the case of Columba. If Ninian himself did indeed go to Rome a generation or more before Columbanus left for Francia, and if he is rightly identified with Finnian or Uinniau, then one of Columbanus' authority figures had already spent time on the continent. And the Irishmen returning from Rome in the *Life of Samson* might provide a further example of such contacts – indeed they may strengthen the case for believing in the stories of Roman pilgrimage in the Irish hagiography. As for Samson himself, he shows that individuals from the Irish Sea province were not only crossing to western Gaul, but were

---

[23] The potential significance of Vinnian for understanding religious life at Whithorn was noted by Hill 1997, 15-16, though without identifying Vinnian and Ninian.

also influencing Frankish politics more than quarter of a century before Columbanus entered the Merovingian world.

Choosing between the options

The late chronology for Ninian would thus place him, and his continental connections, in a radically different context from that implied by the early chronology. In the first, one has to set him against the work of Germanus, Palladius and Patrick – that is to set him in a context of the pastoral concerns of bishops, perhaps even in that of the drive against Pelagianism, and, more important, of missionary work, at a time that the West Roman Empire was failing. This, of course, would sort well with Ninian's evangelisation of the southern Picts. The supposed period of instruction in Rome could be put alongside the interests of pope Celestine, and his despatch of Palladius – and it might be paralleled with time spent in Rome by Ailbhe. The dedication of the church at Whithorn to Martin would probably have to be seen as a later development.

This would not have to be the case if one placed Ninian's *floruit* in the sixth century. In this reconstruction, however, rather than belonging to the last decades of Roman Britain, Ninian would best be seen as a figure in a cultural world that united western Britain and Ireland with Francia and beyond. He could be situated directly between Gildas and Columbanus. The dominant features of this world are monastic and penitential. The mission to the southern Picts would cease to belong to the age of pope Celestine, but rather become a parallel to Columba's work among their more northerly brothers. Indeed, if Ninian is to be identified with Finnian of Moville and Clonard, he would become Columba's immediate predecessor in missionary work (Clancy 2001; Dumville 1984, 213-4 on a group of possible identifications), although it should be noted that Bede describes the conversion of the southern Picts as taking place a long time before that of their northern brothers (Bede *Historia Ecclesiastica* III 4). In addition Ninian's journey to Rome – or perhaps that of one of his pupils – would belong to a cluster of pilgrimages apparently made by Irishmen in the mid-sixth century. And it might be added that according to the hagiography two of these pilgrimages took in the shrine of Martin at Tours.
Neither of these reconstructions is obviously more plausible than the other. Of course, there are other possible contexts: what would happen if one tried to place Ninian's career in the transitional period made up of the very last years of the fifth century and the first of the sixth, despite the insecurities of the time? This might gain some support from the earliest inscribed stones of the Whithorn region, if they do indeed begin after the period 450-80, as suggested by Jeremy Knight, though this is questionable (Knight 1996, 112).[24] Unfortunately we do not have the evidence to attempt such a reconstruction, and that itself may be significant. Ultimately, it may be that the solution to the identification of Ninian's floruit will lie in the inscribed stones and the archaeology of Whithorn itself, though at present Peter Hill's dating of the end of Phase 1 of the monastery as c550 could fit either an early or a late Ninian: it would merely imply that the saint played a different role in its origin or development.

As things stand, each of the two reconstructions has points to recommend it. Each also raises difficulties: if Ninian and Finnian really were one and the same man, one would want to know how it was that this was forgotten – for Bede would surely have been delighted to present the saint as Irish if he could have done so, even by a sleight of hand (Barrow 2004, 7-10 sets out the problems). What the two reconstructions do show, however, is that cultural and religious relations between western Britain and the continent changed radically during the fifth and sixth centuries. Indeed, comparison of these two possible contexts for Ninian serves to draw out the developments. It is conceivable that both contexts are relevant to the history of Whithorn: that its Christian origins belong in the first, but that Ninian himself belongs in the second. If only we could be sure where he belonged, he would enrich our understanding not just of Whithorn, but of the wider world of relations between the western seabord of Britain, Gaul and Rome.

---

[24] Forsyth 2005, 115-7, would, however, tend to push the start date earlier.

References

Primary sources:

Bede (ed C Plummer 1896) *Historia Ecclesiastica Gentis Anglorum, Baedae Opera Historica.* Oxford.

Bede (ed C W Jones 1975a) *Kalendarium sive Martyrologium, Beda Venerabilis, Opera Didascalica, Corpus Christianorum* (Series Latina CXXIII A). Turnhout.

Bede (ed C W Jones 1975b) *De Temporibus, Beda Venerabilis, Opera Didascalica, Corpus Christianorum* (Series Latina CXXIII A). Turnhout.

Bieler, L, (ed) 1975 *The Irish Penitentials.* Dublin.

Columbanus (ed G S M Walker 1970) *Sancti Columbani Opera.* Dublin.

Constantius of Lyons (ed R Borius 1965) *Vita Germani, Sources Chrétiennes* 112. Paris.

Council of Paris (556-73) (ed J Gaudemet and B Basdevant 1989), *Les canons des conciles mérovingiens (VIe-VIIe siècles),* vol. 2, *Sources Chrétiennes* 354, pp 412-25. Paris.

Council of Tours (461) (ed C Munier 1963) *Concilia Galliae A.314-A.506,* pp 142-9. Turnhout.

Gerontios (ed D Gorce 1962) *Vita Melaniae* in *Vie de sainte Mélanie.* Paris.

Gildas (ed M Winterbottom 1978) *De Excidio Britonum* in *Gildas, The Ruin of Britain and other documents.* Chichester.

Gregory of Tours (ed B Krusch & W Levison 1951) *Decem Libri Historiarum* in *Monumenta Germaniae Historica, Scriptores Rerum Merovingicarum* I, 1. Hannover.

Jonas (ed B Krusch 1905) *Vita Columbani* in *Monumenta Germaniae Historica, Scriptores rerum Germanicarum.* Hannover.

Jordanes (ed F Giunta & A Grillone 1991) *Getica* in *Iordanis De Origine Actibusque Getarum.* Rome.

Miracula Nynie Episcopi (ed K Strecker 1923) *Monumenta Germaniae Historica, Poetae Latini Aevi Carolini* IV, 3, pp 943-61. Berlin.

Muirchú, *Vita Patricii* (ed L Bieler 1979) *The Patrician Texts in the Book of Armagh.* Dublin.

Patrick (ed D R Howlett 1994) *The Book of Letters of saint Patrick the bishop.* Dublin.

Procopius (ed H B Dewing 1914-28) *Wars,* 5 vols. Cambridge, Mass.

Prosper (ed T Mommsen 1892) *Chronicon* in *Monumenta Germaniae Historica, Auctores Antiquissimi* IX, *Chronica Minora* I, 385-485. Berlin.

Sidonius Apollinaris (ed A Loyen 1960-70), 3 vols. Paris.

Venantius Fortunatus (ed S Quesnel 2002) *Vita Martini* in *Venance Fortunat, Œuvres* IV, *La vie de saint Martin.* Paris.

Vita s. Albei (ed W W Heist 1965) in *Vitae Sanctorum Hiberniae.* Brussels.

Vita s. Columbae de Tír dá Glas (ed W W Heist 1965) in *Vitae Sanctorum Hiberniae.* Brussels.

Vita s. Finniani (ed W W Heist) 1965 in *Vitae Sanctorum Hiberniae.* Brussels.

Vita Genovefae (ed B Krusch 1896) in *Monumenta Germaniae Historica, Scriptores Rerum Merovingicarum* III, pp. 204-238. Hannover.

Vita Gildae auctore monacho Ruiensi (ed H Williams 1889) in *Two Lives of Gildas, Cymrodorion Record Series).*

Vita s. Mochtei (ed W W Heist 1965) in *Vitae Sanctorum Hiberniae.* Brussels.

Vita Samsonis (ed P Flobert 1997) in *La Vie ancienne de Saint Samson de Dol.* Paris.

Vita s. Tigernachi (ed W W Heist 1965) in *Vitae Sanctorum Hiberniae.* Brussels.

Secondary works:

Barrow, G 2004 *Saint Ninian and Pictomania* (The Twelfth Whithorn Lecture 2003). Friends of the Whithorn Trust, Whithorn.

Bassett, S 1989 *The Origins of Anglo-Saxon Kingdoms.* Leicester.

Blair, J, 2005 *The Church in Anglo-Saxon Society.* Oxford.

Chadwick, N K 1955 *Poetry and Letters in Early Christian Gaul.* London.

Charles-Edwards, T M 1993 'Palladius, Prosper, and Leo the Great: mission and primatial authority', *in* Dumville, 1-12.

Charles-Edwards, T M 1997 'The penitential of Columbanus', *in* Lapidge (ed), 217-39.

Charles-Edwards, T M 2000 *Early Christian Ireland*. Cambridge.

Clancy, T O 2001 'The real St Ninian', *Innes Review* 52, 1-28.

Dark, K R (ed) 1996 *External Contacts and the Economy of Late Roman and Post-Roman Britain*. Woodbridge.

Dumville, D N 1984 'Gildas and Uinniau', *in* Lapidge & Dumville (eds), 207-14. Woodbridge.

Dumville, D N 1993 *Saint Patrick AD 493-1993*. Woodbridge.

Forsyth, K 2005 *'HIC MEMORIA PERPETUA*: the inscribed stones of sub-Roman southern Scotland', *in* Foster, S & Cross, M (eds) *'Able minds and practised hands': Scotland's Early Medieval Sculpture in the 21ˢᵗ Century*, 113-34. Oxbow, Oxford (=Society for Medieval Archaeology Monograph series).

Galliou, P & Jones, M 1991 *The Bretons*. Oxford.

Handley, M 2001 'The Origins of Christian Commemoration in late antique Britain' *Early Medieval Europe* 10, 177-199.

Hanson, R P C 1968 *Saint Patrick, his origins and career*. Oxford.

Heinzelmann, M & Poulin, J-C 1986 *Les vies anciennes de sainte Geneviève de Paris*. Paris.

Herren, M W 1990 'Gildas and early British monasticism', *in* Bammesberger & Wollmann (eds) *Britain 400-600: Language and History*, 65-78. Heidelberg.

Hill, P 1997 *Whithorn and St Ninian: The Excavation of a Monastic Town 1984-91*, Sutton/Whithorn Trust, Stroud.

Hill, P 2001 'Whithorn, Latinus and the origins of Christianity in Northern Britain', *in* Hamerow, H & MacGregor, A (eds) *Image and Power in the Archaeology of Early Medieval Britain: Essays in Honour of Rosemary Cramp*, 23-32. Oxbow Books, Oxford.

Kerlouegan, F 1987 *Le De Excidio Britanniae de Gildas. Les destinées de la culture latine dans l'île de Bretagne au VIe siècle*. Paris.

Knight, J K 1996 'Seasoned with salt: insular-Gallic contacts in the early memorial stones and cross slabs' *in* Dark (ed), 109-20.

Lapidge, M 1984 'Gildas's education and the Latin culture of sub-Roman Britain' *in* Lapidge & Dumville (eds), 27-50.

Lapidge, M 1996 'Aediluulf and the School of York', *in* Lapidge, M *Anglo-Latin Literature 600-899*, 381-98. London.

Lapidge, M (ed) 1997 *Columbanus: Studies on the Latin Writings*. Woodbridge.

Lapidge, M & Dumville, D N (eds) 1984 *Gildas: New Approaches*. Woodbridge.

Meyer, W 1904 *Die Legende des h. Albanus, des Protomartyr Angliae in Texten vor Beda, Abhandlungen der königlichen Gesellschaft der Wissenschaften zu Göttingen* (philologisch-historische Klasse VIII, 1). Berlin.

Orchard, A 2000 'Wish you were here: Alcuin's courtly poetry and the boys back home', *in* Rees Jones, S, Marks, R, & Minnis, A J (eds) *Courts and Regions in Medieval Europe*, 21-43. York.

Orton, F, Wood, I N, & Lees, C 2007 *Fragments of History*. Manchester.

Shanzer, D 1998 'Dating the baptism of Clovis: the bishop of Vienne vs the bishop of Tours', *Early Medieval Europe* 7, 29-57.

Shanzer, D & Wood, I 2002 *Avitus of Vienne: Letters and Selected Prose*. Liverpool,

Sharpe, R 1984 'Gildas as father of the Church' *in* Lapidge & Dumville (eds), 193-205.

Sharpe, R 2001 'The late antique Passio of St Alban' *in* Henig, M & Lindley, P (eds) *Alban and St Albans, Roman and Medieval Architecture, Art and Archaeology*, 30-7. British Archaeological Association, Conference Transactions 24.

Stancliffe, C 1997 'The thirteen sermons attributed to Columbanus' *in* Lapidge (ed), 93-202.

Thomas, C 1994 *And Shall These Mute Stones Speak?*. Cardiff.

Thompson, E A 1980a 'Procopius on Brittia and Britannia', *Classical Quarterly* 74, 498-507.

Thompson, E A 1980b 'St Patrick and Coroticus', *J of Theological Studies*, new series 31, 12-27.

Thompson, E A 1985 *Who was St Patrick?*. Woodbridge.

Van Dam, R 1993 *Saints and their Miracles in Late Antique Gaul*. Princeton.

van Egmond, W S 2006 *Conversing with the Saints: Communication in Pre-Carolingian Hagiography from Auxerre*. Brepols.

Wilmott, T 1997 *Birdoswald. Excavations of a Roman fort on Hadrian's Wall and its successor settlements: 1987-9*. London.

Wood, I N 1984 'The End of Roman Britain: continental evidence and parallels' *in* Lapidge & Dumville (eds), 1-25.

Wood, I N 1987 'The Fall of the Western Empire and the end of Roman Britain', *Britannia* 18, 251-62.

Wood, I N 1988 'Forgery in Merovingian Hagiography', *in Fälschungen im Mittelalter*, vol 5, *Fingierte Briefe, Frömmigkeit und Fälschung, Realienfälschungen*, 369-84. Hannover.

Wood, I N 1992 'Continuity or calamity: the constraints of literary models', *in* Drinkwater, J & Elton, H (eds) *Fifth-century Gaul: a crisis of identity?*, 99-120. Cambridge.

Wood, I N 1998 'Jonas, the Merovingians, and Pope Honorius', *in* Murray, A C (ed) *After Rome's Fall*. Toronto.

Wood, I N 2003 'Ruthwell: Contextual Searches', *in* Karkov, C & Orton, F (eds) *Theorizing Anglo-Saxon Stone Sculpture*, 104-30. Morgantown.

Wood, I N 2004 'The Final Phase', *in* Todd, M (ed) *A Companion to Roman Britain*, 428-42. Oxford.

Wood, I N 2006 'The Franks and Papal Theology', *in* Chazelle, C & Cubitt, C (eds) *The Crisis of the Oecumene: the Three Chapters and the Failed Quest for Unity in the Sixth-Century Mediterranean*, 223-42. Turnhout.

Wooding, J M 1996 'Cargoes in trade along the western seaboard', *in* Dark (ed), 67-82.

Wright, N 1984 'Gildas's Prose Style and its Origins', *in* Lapidge & Dumville (eds), 107-28.

Wright, N 1997 'Columbanus's *Epistulae*' *in* Lapidge (ed), 29-92.